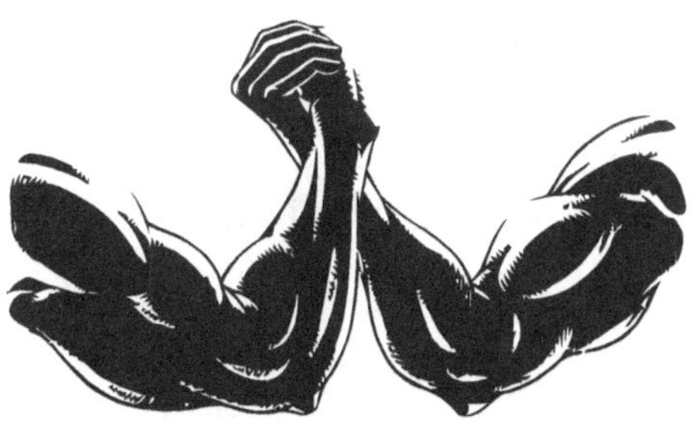

WORKOUT
Log Book

NAME: ___________________________

PHONE: ___________________________

HOW TO USE THIS BOOK

1. Date Tracker/Day and Time
2. Track Workout Types
3. Track Water Intake
4. Track Vitamins/Supplements
5. Track Nutrition
6. Track Strength Training
7. Track Moods
8. To Do/Notes
9. Weight

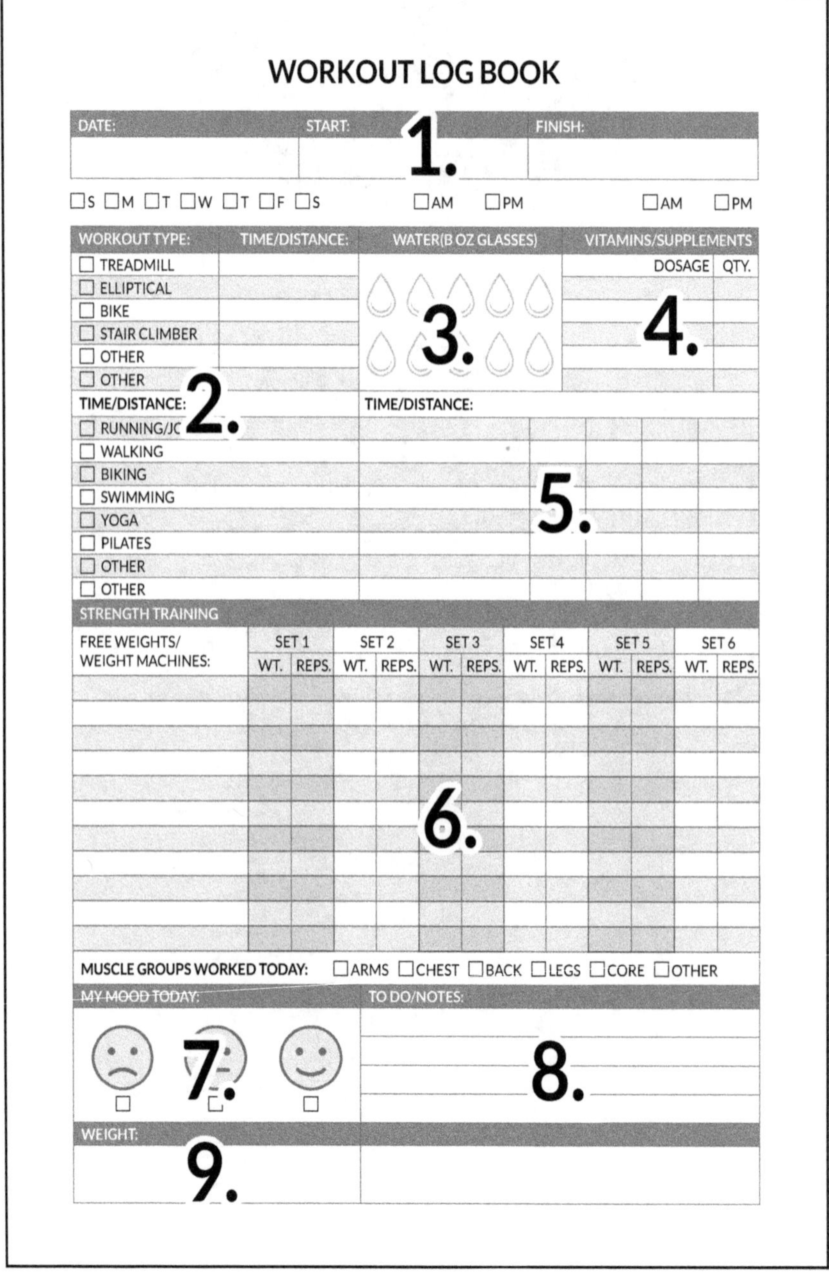

WORKOUT LOG BOOK

DATE:	START:	FINISH:

☐ S ☐ M ☐ T ☐ W ☐ T ☐ F ☐ S   ☐ AM   ☐ PM   ☐ AM   ☐ PM

WORKOUT TYPE:	TIME/DISTANCE:	WATER (B OZ GLASSES)	VITAMINS/SUPPLEMENTS	DOSAGE	QTY.
☐ TREADMILL					
☐ ELLIPTICAL					
☐ BIKE					
☐ STAIR CLIMBER					
☐ OTHER					
☐ OTHER					

TIME/DISTANCE: **TIME/DISTANCE:**

☐ RUNNING/JOG				
☐ WALKING				
☐ BIKING				
☐ SWIMMING				
☐ YOGA				
☐ PILATES				
☐ OTHER				
☐ OTHER				

STRENGTH TRAINING

FREE WEIGHTS/ WEIGHT MACHINES:	SET 1		SET 2		SET 3		SET 4		SET 5		SET 6	
	WT.	REPS.	WT.	REPS.	WT.	REPS.	WT.	REPS.	WT.	REPS.	WT.	REPS.

MUSCLE GROUPS WORKED TODAY: ☐ ARMS ☐ CHEST ☐ BACK ☐ LEGS ☐ CORE ☐ OTHER

MY MOOD TODAY:	TO DO/NOTES:
☹ ☐ 😐 ☐ 🙂 ☐	

WEIGHT:

WORKOUT LOG BOOK

DATE:	START:	FINISH:

☐ S ☐ M ☐ T ☐ W ☐ T ☐ F ☐ S   ☐ AM   ☐ PM   ☐ AM   ☐ PM

WORKOUT TYPE:	TIME/DISTANCE:	WATER(B OZ GLASSES)	VITAMINS/SUPPLEMENTS	
			DOSAGE	QTY.
☐ TREADMILL				
☐ ELLIPTICAL				
☐ BIKE				
☐ STAIR CLIMBER				
☐ OTHER				
☐ OTHER				

TIME/DISTANCE: **TIME/DISTANCE:**

Activity				
☐ RUNNING/JOG				
☐ WALKING				
☐ BIKING				
☐ SWIMMING				
☐ YOGA				
☐ PILATES				
☐ OTHER				
☐ OTHER				

STRENGTH TRAINING

FREE WEIGHTS/ WEIGHT MACHINES:	SET 1		SET 2		SET 3		SET 4		SET 5		SET 6	
	WT.	REPS.	WT.	REPS.	WT.	REPS.	WT.	REPS.	WT.	REPS.	WT.	REPS.

MUSCLE GROUPS WORKED TODAY: ☐ ARMS ☐ CHEST ☐ BACK ☐ LEGS ☐ CORE ☐ OTHER

MY MOOD TODAY: **TO DO/NOTES:**

☐   ☐   ☐

WEIGHT:

WORKOUT LOG BOOK

DATE:	START:	FINISH:

☐ S ☐ M ☐ T ☐ W ☐ T ☐ F ☐ S   ☐ AM ☐ PM   ☐ AM ☐ PM

WORKOUT TYPE:	TIME/DISTANCE:	WATER(B OZ GLASSES)	VITAMINS/SUPPLEMENTS	
			DOSAGE	QTY.
☐ TREADMILL				
☐ ELLIPTICAL				
☐ BIKE				
☐ STAIR CLIMBER				
☐ OTHER				
☐ OTHER				

TIME/DISTANCE: **TIME/DISTANCE:**

☐ RUNNING/JOG					
☐ WALKING					
☐ BIKING					
☐ SWIMMING					
☐ YOGA					
☐ PILATES					
☐ OTHER					
☐ OTHER					

STRENGTH TRAINING

FREE WEIGHTS/ WEIGHT MACHINES:	SET 1		SET 2		SET 3		SET 4		SET 5		SET 6	
	WT.	REPS.	WT.	REPS.	WT.	REPS.	WT.	REPS.	WT.	REPS.	WT.	REPS.

MUSCLE GROUPS WORKED TODAY: ☐ ARMS ☐ CHEST ☐ BACK ☐ LEGS ☐ CORE ☐ OTHER

MY MOOD TODAY: **TO DO/NOTES:**

☐   ☐   ☐

WEIGHT:

WORKOUT LOG BOOK

DATE:	START:	FINISH:

☐S ☐M ☐T ☐W ☐T ☐F ☐S   ☐AM ☐PM   ☐AM ☐PM

WORKOUT TYPE:	TIME/DISTANCE:	WATER(B OZ GLASSES)	VITAMINS/SUPPLEMENTS

			DOSAGE	QTY.
☐ TREADMILL				
☐ ELLIPTICAL				
☐ BIKE				
☐ STAIR CLIMBER				
☐ OTHER				
☐ OTHER				

TIME/DISTANCE: **TIME/DISTANCE:**

| ☐ RUNNING/JOG |
| ☐ WALKING |
| ☐ BIKING |
| ☐ SWIMMING |
| ☐ YOGA |
| ☐ PILATES |
| ☐ OTHER |
| ☐ OTHER |

STRENGTH TRAINING

FREE WEIGHTS/ WEIGHT MACHINES:	SET 1		SET 2		SET 3		SET 4		SET 5		SET 6	
	WT.	REPS.	WT.	REPS.	WT.	REPS.	WT.	REPS.	WT.	REPS.	WT.	REPS.

MUSCLE GROUPS WORKED TODAY: ☐ARMS ☐CHEST ☐BACK ☐LEGS ☐CORE ☐OTHER

MY MOOD TODAY:	TO DO/NOTES:
☐ ☐ ☐	

WEIGHT:

WORKOUT LOG BOOK

DATE:	START:	FINISH:

☐ S ☐ M ☐ T ☐ W ☐ T ☐ F ☐ S   ☐ AM ☐ PM   ☐ AM ☐ PM

WORKOUT TYPE:	TIME/DISTANCE:	WATER(B OZ GLASSES)	VITAMINS/SUPPLEMENTS	
☐ TREADMILL			DOSAGE	QTY.
☐ ELLIPTICAL				
☐ BIKE				
☐ STAIR CLIMBER				
☐ OTHER				
☐ OTHER				

TIME/DISTANCE:

TIME/DISTANCE:

☐ RUNNING/JOG					
☐ WALKING					
☐ BIKING					
☐ SWIMMING					
☐ YOGA					
☐ PILATES					
☐ OTHER					
☐ OTHER					

STRENGTH TRAINING

FREE WEIGHTS/ WEIGHT MACHINES:	SET 1		SET 2		SET 3		SET 4		SET 5		SET 6	
	WT.	REPS.	WT.	REPS.	WT.	REPS.	WT.	REPS.	WT.	REPS.	WT.	REPS.

MUSCLE GROUPS WORKED TODAY: ☐ ARMS ☐ CHEST ☐ BACK ☐ LEGS ☐ CORE ☐ OTHER

MY MOOD TODAY:	TO DO/NOTES:
☐ ☐ ☐	

WEIGHT:

WORKOUT LOG BOOK

DATE:	START:	FINISH:

☐ S ☐ M ☐ T ☐ W ☐ T ☐ F ☐ S ☐ AM ☐ PM ☐ AM ☐ PM

WORKOUT TYPE:	TIME/DISTANCE:	WATER(B OZ GLASSES)	VITAMINS/SUPPLEMENTS	
			DOSAGE	QTY.
☐ TREADMILL				
☐ ELLIPTICAL				
☐ BIKE				
☐ STAIR CLIMBER				
☐ OTHER				
☐ OTHER				

TIME/DISTANCE: **TIME/DISTANCE:**

| ☐ RUNNING/JOG |
| ☐ WALKING |
| ☐ BIKING |
| ☐ SWIMMING |
| ☐ YOGA |
| ☐ PILATES |
| ☐ OTHER |
| ☐ OTHER |

STRENGTH TRAINING

FREE WEIGHTS/ WEIGHT MACHINES:	SET 1		SET 2		SET 3		SET 4		SET 5		SET 6	
	WT.	REPS.	WT.	REPS.	WT.	REPS.	WT.	REPS.	WT.	REPS.	WT.	REPS.

MUSCLE GROUPS WORKED TODAY: ☐ARMS ☐CHEST ☐BACK ☐LEGS ☐CORE ☐OTHER

MY MOOD TODAY:

TO DO/NOTES:

WEIGHT:

WORKOUT LOG BOOK

DATE:	START:	FINISH:

☐ S ☐ M ☐ T ☐ W ☐ T ☐ F ☐ S   ☐ AM ☐ PM   ☐ AM ☐ PM

WORKOUT TYPE:	TIME/DISTANCE:	WATER(B OZ GLASSES)	VITAMINS/SUPPLEMENTS	
			DOSAGE	QTY.
☐ TREADMILL				
☐ ELLIPTICAL				
☐ BIKE				
☐ STAIR CLIMBER				
☐ OTHER				
☐ OTHER				

TIME/DISTANCE:

TIME/DISTANCE:

☐ RUNNING/JOG					
☐ WALKING					
☐ BIKING					
☐ SWIMMING					
☐ YOGA					
☐ PILATES					
☐ OTHER					
☐ OTHER					

STRENGTH TRAINING

FREE WEIGHTS/ WEIGHT MACHINES:	SET 1		SET 2		SET 3		SET 4		SET 5		SET 6	
	WT.	REPS.	WT.	REPS.	WT.	REPS.	WT.	REPS.	WT.	REPS.	WT.	REPS.

MUSCLE GROUPS WORKED TODAY: ☐ ARMS ☐ CHEST ☐ BACK ☐ LEGS ☐ CORE ☐ OTHER

MY MOOD TODAY:	TO DO/NOTES:
☐ ☐ ☐	

WEIGHT:

WORKOUT LOG BOOK

DATE:	START:	FINISH:

☐S ☐M ☐T ☐W ☐T ☐F ☐S   ☐AM   ☐PM   ☐AM   ☐PM

WORKOUT TYPE:	TIME/DISTANCE:	WATER(B OZ GLASSES)	VITAMINS/SUPPLEMENTS	
			DOSAGE	QTY.
☐ TREADMILL				
☐ ELLIPTICAL				
☐ BIKE				
☐ STAIR CLIMBER				
☐ OTHER				
☐ OTHER				

TIME/DISTANCE: **TIME/DISTANCE:**

☐ RUNNING/JOG					
☐ WALKING					
☐ BIKING					
☐ SWIMMING					
☐ YOGA					
☐ PILATES					
☐ OTHER					
☐ OTHER					

STRENGTH TRAINING

FREE WEIGHTS/ WEIGHT MACHINES:	SET 1		SET 2		SET 3		SET 4		SET 5		SET 6	
	WT.	REPS.	WT.	REPS.	WT.	REPS.	WT.	REPS.	WT.	REPS.	WT.	REPS.

MUSCLE GROUPS WORKED TODAY: ☐ARMS ☐CHEST ☐BACK ☐LEGS ☐CORE ☐OTHER

MY MOOD TODAY: **TO DO/NOTES:**

☐   ☐   ☐

WEIGHT:

WORKOUT LOG BOOK

DATE:	START:	FINISH:

☐ S ☐ M ☐ T ☐ W ☐ T ☐ F ☐ S   ☐ AM ☐ PM   ☐ AM ☐ PM

WORKOUT TYPE:	TIME/DISTANCE:	WATER(B OZ GLASSES)	VITAMINS/SUPPLEMENTS	
			DOSAGE	QTY.
☐ TREADMILL				
☐ ELLIPTICAL				
☐ BIKE				
☐ STAIR CLIMBER				
☐ OTHER				
☐ OTHER				

TIME/DISTANCE:

TIME/DISTANCE:

RUNNING/JOG					
☐ RUNNING/JOG					
☐ WALKING					
☐ BIKING					
☐ SWIMMING					
☐ YOGA					
☐ PILATES					
☐ OTHER					
☐ OTHER					

STRENGTH TRAINING

FREE WEIGHTS/ WEIGHT MACHINES:	SET 1		SET 2		SET 3		SET 4		SET 5		SET 6	
	WT.	REPS.	WT.	REPS.	WT.	REPS.	WT.	REPS.	WT.	REPS.	WT.	REPS.

MUSCLE GROUPS WORKED TODAY: ☐ ARMS ☐ CHEST ☐ BACK ☐ LEGS ☐ CORE ☐ OTHER

MY MOOD TODAY:

☐   ☐   ☐

TO DO/NOTES:

WEIGHT:

WORKOUT LOG BOOK

DATE:	START:	FINISH:

☐ S ☐ M ☐ T ☐ W ☐ T ☐ F ☐ S   ☐ AM   ☐ PM   ☐ AM   ☐ PM

WORKOUT TYPE:	TIME/DISTANCE:	WATER(B OZ GLASSES)	VITAMINS/SUPPLEMENTS	
			DOSAGE	QTY.
☐ TREADMILL				
☐ ELLIPTICAL				
☐ BIKE				
☐ STAIR CLIMBER				
☐ OTHER				
☐ OTHER				

TIME/DISTANCE: **TIME/DISTANCE:**

☐ RUNNING/JOG	
☐ WALKING	
☐ BIKING	
☐ SWIMMING	
☐ YOGA	
☐ PILATES	
☐ OTHER	
☐ OTHER	

STRENGTH TRAINING

FREE WEIGHTS/ WEIGHT MACHINES:	SET 1		SET 2		SET 3		SET 4		SET 5		SET 6	
	WT.	REPS.	WT.	REPS.	WT.	REPS.	WT.	REPS.	WT.	REPS.	WT.	REPS.

MUSCLE GROUPS WORKED TODAY: ☐ ARMS ☐ CHEST ☐ BACK ☐ LEGS ☐ CORE ☐ OTHER

MY MOOD TODAY:	TO DO/NOTES:
☐ ☐ ☐	

WEIGHT:

WORKOUT LOG BOOK

DATE:	START:	FINISH:

☐ S ☐ M ☐ T ☐ W ☐ T ☐ F ☐ S   ☐ AM   ☐ PM   ☐ AM   ☐ PM

WORKOUT TYPE:	TIME/DISTANCE:	WATER(B OZ GLASSES)	VITAMINS/SUPPLEMENTS	
			DOSAGE	QTY.
☐ TREADMILL				
☐ ELLIPTICAL				
☐ BIKE				
☐ STAIR CLIMBER				
☐ OTHER				
☐ OTHER				

TIME/DISTANCE: **TIME/DISTANCE:**

☐ RUNNING/JOG					
☐ WALKING					
☐ BIKING					
☐ SWIMMING					
☐ YOGA					
☐ PILATES					
☐ OTHER					
☐ OTHER					

STRENGTH TRAINING

FREE WEIGHTS/ WEIGHT MACHINES:	SET 1		SET 2		SET 3		SET 4		SET 5		SET 6	
	WT.	REPS.	WT.	REPS.	WT.	REPS.	WT.	REPS.	WT.	REPS.	WT.	REPS.

MUSCLE GROUPS WORKED TODAY: ☐ ARMS ☐ CHEST ☐ BACK ☐ LEGS ☐ CORE ☐ OTHER

MY MOOD TODAY:	TO DO/NOTES:
☐ ☐ ☐	

WEIGHT:

WORKOUT LOG BOOK

DATE:	START:	FINISH:

☐S ☐M ☐T ☐W ☐T ☐F ☐S   ☐AM ☐PM   ☐AM ☐PM

WORKOUT TYPE:	TIME/DISTANCE:	WATER(8 OZ GLASSES)	VITAMINS/SUPPLEMENTS	
			DOSAGE	QTY.
☐ TREADMILL				
☐ ELLIPTICAL				
☐ BIKE				
☐ STAIR CLIMBER				
☐ OTHER				
☐ OTHER				

TIME/DISTANCE:	TIME/DISTANCE:					
☐ RUNNING/JOG						
☐ WALKING						
☐ BIKING						
☐ SWIMMING						
☐ YOGA						
☐ PILATES						
☐ OTHER						
☐ OTHER						

STRENGTH TRAINING

FREE WEIGHTS/ WEIGHT MACHINES:	SET 1		SET 2		SET 3		SET 4		SET 5		SET 6	
	WT.	REPS.	WT.	REPS.	WT.	REPS.	WT.	REPS.	WT.	REPS.	WT.	REPS.

MUSCLE GROUPS WORKED TODAY: ☐ARMS ☐CHEST ☐BACK ☐LEGS ☐CORE ☐OTHER

MY MOOD TODAY:	TO DO/NOTES:

☐   ☐   ☐

WEIGHT:

WORKOUT LOG BOOK

DATE:	START:	FINISH:

☐ S ☐ M ☐ T ☐ W ☐ T ☐ F ☐ S   ☐ AM   ☐ PM   ☐ AM   ☐ PM

WORKOUT TYPE:	TIME/DISTANCE:	WATER(B OZ GLASSES)	VITAMINS/SUPPLEMENTS	
			DOSAGE	QTY.
☐ TREADMILL				
☐ ELLIPTICAL				
☐ BIKE				
☐ STAIR CLIMBER				
☐ OTHER				
☐ OTHER				

TIME/DISTANCE: **TIME/DISTANCE:**

RUNNING/JOG etc.				
☐ RUNNING/JOG				
☐ WALKING				
☐ BIKING				
☐ SWIMMING				
☐ YOGA				
☐ PILATES				
☐ OTHER				
☐ OTHER				

STRENGTH TRAINING

FREE WEIGHTS/ WEIGHT MACHINES:	SET 1		SET 2		SET 3		SET 4		SET 5		SET 6	
	WT.	REPS.	WT.	REPS.	WT.	REPS.	WT.	REPS.	WT.	REPS.	WT.	REPS.

MUSCLE GROUPS WORKED TODAY: ☐ ARMS ☐ CHEST ☐ BACK ☐ LEGS ☐ CORE ☐ OTHER

MY MOOD TODAY:	TO DO/NOTES:
☹ ☐ 😐 ☐ 🙂 ☐	

WEIGHT:

WORKOUT LOG BOOK

DATE:	START:	FINISH:

☐ S ☐ M ☐ T ☐ W ☐ T ☐ F ☐ S   ☐ AM   ☐ PM   ☐ AM   ☐ PM

WORKOUT TYPE:	TIME/DISTANCE:	WATER(B OZ GLASSES)	VITAMINS/SUPPLEMENTS	
			DOSAGE	QTY.
☐ TREADMILL				
☐ ELLIPTICAL				
☐ BIKE				
☐ STAIR CLIMBER				
☐ OTHER				
☐ OTHER				

TIME/DISTANCE: **TIME/DISTANCE:**

☐ RUNNING/JOG					
☐ WALKING					
☐ BIKING					
☐ SWIMMING					
☐ YOGA					
☐ PILATES					
☐ OTHER					
☐ OTHER					

STRENGTH TRAINING

FREE WEIGHTS/ WEIGHT MACHINES:	SET 1		SET 2		SET 3		SET 4		SET 5		SET 6	
	WT.	REPS.	WT.	REPS.	WT.	REPS.	WT.	REPS.	WT.	REPS.	WT.	REPS.

MUSCLE GROUPS WORKED TODAY: ☐ ARMS ☐ CHEST ☐ BACK ☐ LEGS ☐ CORE ☐ OTHER

MY MOOD TODAY:	TO DO/NOTES:
☹ ☐ 😐 ☐ 🙂 ☐	

WEIGHT:	

WORKOUT LOG BOOK

DATE:	START:	FINISH:

☐ S ☐ M ☐ T ☐ W ☐ T ☐ F ☐ S   ☐ AM ☐ PM   ☐ AM ☐ PM

WORKOUT TYPE:	TIME/DISTANCE:	WATER (8 OZ GLASSES)	VITAMINS/SUPPLEMENTS	
			DOSAGE	QTY.
☐ TREADMILL				
☐ ELLIPTICAL				
☐ BIKE				
☐ STAIR CLIMBER				
☐ OTHER				
☐ OTHER				

TIME/DISTANCE:

TIME/DISTANCE:

☐ RUNNING/JOG						
☐ WALKING						
☐ BIKING						
☐ SWIMMING						
☐ YOGA						
☐ PILATES						
☐ OTHER						
☐ OTHER						

STRENGTH TRAINING

FREE WEIGHTS/ WEIGHT MACHINES:	SET 1		SET 2		SET 3		SET 4		SET 5		SET 6	
	WT.	REPS.	WT.	REPS.	WT.	REPS.	WT.	REPS.	WT.	REPS.	WT.	REPS.

MUSCLE GROUPS WORKED TODAY: ☐ ARMS ☐ CHEST ☐ BACK ☐ LEGS ☐ CORE ☐ OTHER

MY MOOD TODAY:	TO DO/NOTES:
☐ ☐ ☐	

WEIGHT:

WORKOUT LOG BOOK

DATE:	START:	FINISH:

☐ S ☐ M ☐ T ☐ W ☐ T ☐ F ☐ S   ☐ AM   ☐ PM   ☐ AM   ☐ PM

WORKOUT TYPE:	TIME/DISTANCE:	WATER(B OZ GLASSES)	VITAMINS/SUPPLEMENTS	
			DOSAGE	QTY.
☐ TREADMILL				
☐ ELLIPTICAL				
☐ BIKE				
☐ STAIR CLIMBER				
☐ OTHER				
☐ OTHER				

TIME/DISTANCE: **TIME/DISTANCE:**

☐ RUNNING/JOG						
☐ WALKING						
☐ BIKING						
☐ SWIMMING						
☐ YOGA						
☐ PILATES						
☐ OTHER						
☐ OTHER						

STRENGTH TRAINING

FREE WEIGHTS/ WEIGHT MACHINES:	SET 1		SET 2		SET 3		SET 4		SET 5		SET 6	
	WT.	REPS.	WT.	REPS.	WT.	REPS.	WT.	REPS.	WT.	REPS.	WT.	REPS.

MUSCLE GROUPS WORKED TODAY: ☐ ARMS ☐ CHEST ☐ BACK ☐ LEGS ☐ CORE ☐ OTHER

MY MOOD TODAY:	TO DO/NOTES:
☐ ☐ ☐	

WEIGHT:

WORKOUT LOG BOOK

DATE:	START:	FINISH:

☐ S ☐ M ☐ T ☐ W ☐ T ☐ F ☐ S   ☐ AM   ☐ PM   ☐ AM   ☐ PM

WORKOUT TYPE:	TIME/DISTANCE:	WATER(B OZ GLASSES)	VITAMINS/SUPPLEMENTS

VITAMINS/SUPPLEMENTS	DOSAGE	QTY.

WORKOUT TYPE:
- ☐ TREADMILL
- ☐ ELLIPTICAL
- ☐ BIKE
- ☐ STAIR CLIMBER
- ☐ OTHER
- ☐ OTHER

TIME/DISTANCE:
- ☐ RUNNING/JOG
- ☐ WALKING
- ☐ BIKING
- ☐ SWIMMING
- ☐ YOGA
- ☐ PILATES
- ☐ OTHER
- ☐ OTHER

TIME/DISTANCE:

STRENGTH TRAINING

FREE WEIGHTS/ WEIGHT MACHINES:	SET 1		SET 2		SET 3		SET 4		SET 5		SET 6	
	WT.	REPS.	WT.	REPS.	WT.	REPS.	WT.	REPS.	WT.	REPS.	WT.	REPS.

MUSCLE GROUPS WORKED TODAY: ☐ ARMS ☐ CHEST ☐ BACK ☐ LEGS ☐ CORE ☐ OTHER

MY MOOD TODAY: **TO DO/NOTES:**

☐   ☐   ☐

WEIGHT:

WORKOUT LOG BOOK

DATE:	START:	FINISH:

☐ S ☐ M ☐ T ☐ W ☐ T ☐ F ☐ S ☐ AM ☐ PM ☐ AM ☐ PM

WORKOUT TYPE:	TIME/DISTANCE:	WATER(B OZ GLASSES)	VITAMINS/SUPPLEMENTS	
☐ TREADMILL			DOSAGE	QTY.
☐ ELLIPTICAL				
☐ BIKE				
☐ STAIR CLIMBER				
☐ OTHER				
☐ OTHER				

TIME/DISTANCE:	TIME/DISTANCE:			
☐ RUNNING/JOG				
☐ WALKING				
☐ BIKING				
☐ SWIMMING				
☐ YOGA				
☐ PILATES				
☐ OTHER				
☐ OTHER				

STRENGTH TRAINING

FREE WEIGHTS/ WEIGHT MACHINES:	SET 1		SET 2		SET 3		SET 4		SET 5		SET 6	
	WT.	REPS.	WT.	REPS.	WT.	REPS.	WT.	REPS.	WT.	REPS.	WT.	REPS.

MUSCLE GROUPS WORKED TODAY: ☐ ARMS ☐ CHEST ☐ BACK ☐ LEGS ☐ CORE ☐ OTHER

MY MOOD TODAY:	TO DO/NOTES:
☐ ☐ ☐	

WEIGHT:

WORKOUT LOG BOOK

DATE:	START:	FINISH:

☐ S ☐ M ☐ T ☐ W ☐ T ☐ F ☐ S   ☐ AM   ☐ PM   ☐ AM   ☐ PM

WORKOUT TYPE:	TIME/DISTANCE:	WATER(B OZ GLASSES)	VITAMINS/SUPPLEMENTS		
				DOSAGE	QTY.
☐ TREADMILL					
☐ ELLIPTICAL					
☐ BIKE					
☐ STAIR CLIMBER					
☐ OTHER					
☐ OTHER					

TIME/DISTANCE: **TIME/DISTANCE:**

TIME/DISTANCE:						
☐ RUNNING/JOG						
☐ WALKING						
☐ BIKING						
☐ SWIMMING						
☐ YOGA						
☐ PILATES						
☐ OTHER						
☐ OTHER						

STRENGTH TRAINING

FREE WEIGHTS/ WEIGHT MACHINES:	SET 1		SET 2		SET 3		SET 4		SET 5		SET 6	
	WT.	REPS.	WT.	REPS.	WT.	REPS.	WT.	REPS.	WT.	REPS.	WT.	REPS.

MUSCLE GROUPS WORKED TODAY: ☐ ARMS ☐ CHEST ☐ BACK ☐ LEGS ☐ CORE ☐ OTHER

MY MOOD TODAY:	TO DO/NOTES:
☹ ☐ 😐 ☐ 🙂 ☐	

WEIGHT:

WORKOUT LOG BOOK

DATE:	START:	FINISH:

☐ S ☐ M ☐ T ☐ W ☐ T ☐ F ☐ S   ☐ AM   ☐ PM   ☐ AM   ☐ PM

WORKOUT TYPE:	TIME/DISTANCE:	WATER(B OZ GLASSES)	VITAMINS/SUPPLEMENTS	
			DOSAGE	QTY.
☐ TREADMILL				
☐ ELLIPTICAL				
☐ BIKE				
☐ STAIR CLIMBER				
☐ OTHER				
☐ OTHER				

TIME/DISTANCE:

TIME/DISTANCE:

☐ RUNNING/JOG						
☐ WALKING						
☐ BIKING						
☐ SWIMMING						
☐ YOGA						
☐ PILATES						
☐ OTHER						
☐ OTHER						

STRENGTH TRAINING

FREE WEIGHTS/ WEIGHT MACHINES:	SET 1		SET 2		SET 3		SET 4		SET 5		SET 6	
	WT.	REPS.	WT.	REPS.	WT.	REPS.	WT.	REPS.	WT.	REPS.	WT.	REPS.

MUSCLE GROUPS WORKED TODAY: ☐ ARMS ☐ CHEST ☐ BACK ☐ LEGS ☐ CORE ☐ OTHER

MY MOOD TODAY:

☹ ☐   😐 ☐   🙂 ☐

TO DO/NOTES:

WEIGHT:

WORKOUT LOG BOOK

DATE:	START:	FINISH:

☐ S ☐ M ☐ T ☐ W ☐ T ☐ F ☐ S   ☐ AM   ☐ PM   ☐ AM   ☐ PM

WORKOUT TYPE:	TIME/DISTANCE:	WATER(B OZ GLASSES)	VITAMINS/SUPPLEMENTS	
			DOSAGE	QTY.
☐ TREADMILL				
☐ ELLIPTICAL				
☐ BIKE				
☐ STAIR CLIMBER				
☐ OTHER				
☐ OTHER				

TIME/DISTANCE: **TIME/DISTANCE:**

☐ RUNNING/JOG					
☐ WALKING					
☐ BIKING					
☐ SWIMMING					
☐ YOGA					
☐ PILATES					
☐ OTHER					
☐ OTHER					

STRENGTH TRAINING

FREE WEIGHTS/ WEIGHT MACHINES:	SET 1		SET 2		SET 3		SET 4		SET 5		SET 6	
	WT.	REPS.	WT.	REPS.	WT.	REPS.	WT.	REPS.	WT.	REPS.	WT.	REPS.

MUSCLE GROUPS WORKED TODAY: ☐ ARMS ☐ CHEST ☐ BACK ☐ LEGS ☐ CORE ☐ OTHER

MY MOOD TODAY:	TO DO/NOTES:
☹ ☐ 😐 ☐ ☺ ☐	

WEIGHT:

WORKOUT LOG BOOK

DATE:	START:	FINISH:

☐ S ☐ M ☐ T ☐ W ☐ T ☐ F ☐ S   ☐ AM   ☐ PM   ☐ AM   ☐ PM

WORKOUT TYPE:	TIME/DISTANCE:	WATER(B OZ GLASSES)	VITAMINS/SUPPLEMENTS	
			DOSAGE	QTY.
☐ TREADMILL				
☐ ELLIPTICAL				
☐ BIKE				
☐ STAIR CLIMBER				
☐ OTHER				
☐ OTHER				

TIME/DISTANCE: **TIME/DISTANCE:**

☐ RUNNING/JOG					
☐ WALKING					
☐ BIKING					
☐ SWIMMING					
☐ YOGA					
☐ PILATES					
☐ OTHER					
☐ OTHER					

STRENGTH TRAINING

FREE WEIGHTS/ WEIGHT MACHINES:	SET 1		SET 2		SET 3		SET 4		SET 5		SET 6	
	WT.	REPS.	WT.	REPS.	WT.	REPS.	WT.	REPS.	WT.	REPS.	WT.	REPS.

MUSCLE GROUPS WORKED TODAY: ☐ ARMS ☐ CHEST ☐ BACK ☐ LEGS ☐ CORE ☐ OTHER

MY MOOD TODAY:	TO DO/NOTES:
☹ ☐ 😐 ☐ 🙂 ☐	

WEIGHT:

WORKOUT LOG BOOK

DATE:	START:	FINISH:

☐ S ☐ M ☐ T ☐ W ☐ T ☐ F ☐ S   ☐ AM ☐ PM   ☐ AM ☐ PM

WORKOUT TYPE:	TIME/DISTANCE:	WATER(B OZ GLASSES)	VITAMINS/SUPPLEMENTS	
			DOSAGE	QTY.
☐ TREADMILL				
☐ ELLIPTICAL				
☐ BIKE				
☐ STAIR CLIMBER				
☐ OTHER				
☐ OTHER				

TIME/DISTANCE: **TIME/DISTANCE:**

☐ RUNNING/JOG					
☐ WALKING					
☐ BIKING					
☐ SWIMMING					
☐ YOGA					
☐ PILATES					
☐ OTHER					
☐ OTHER					

STRENGTH TRAINING

FREE WEIGHTS/ WEIGHT MACHINES:	SET 1		SET 2		SET 3		SET 4		SET 5		SET 6	
	WT.	REPS.	WT.	REPS.	WT.	REPS.	WT.	REPS.	WT.	REPS.	WT.	REPS.

MUSCLE GROUPS WORKED TODAY: ☐ ARMS ☐ CHEST ☐ BACK ☐ LEGS ☐ CORE ☐ OTHER

MY MOOD TODAY:

TO DO/NOTES:

☐   ☐   ☐

WEIGHT:

WORKOUT LOG BOOK

DATE:	START:	FINISH:

☐ S ☐ M ☐ T ☐ W ☐ T ☐ F ☐ S   ☐ AM   ☐ PM   ☐ AM   ☐ PM

WORKOUT TYPE:	TIME/DISTANCE:	WATER(B OZ GLASSES)	VITAMINS/SUPPLEMENTS	
			DOSAGE	QTY.
☐ TREADMILL				
☐ ELLIPTICAL				
☐ BIKE				
☐ STAIR CLIMBER				
☐ OTHER				
☐ OTHER				

TIME/DISTANCE: **TIME/DISTANCE:**

RUNNING/JOG	WALKING	BIKING	SWIMMING	YOGA	PILATES	OTHER	OTHER
☐ RUNNING/JOG							
☐ WALKING							
☐ BIKING							
☐ SWIMMING							
☐ YOGA							
☐ PILATES							
☐ OTHER							
☐ OTHER							

STRENGTH TRAINING

FREE WEIGHTS/ WEIGHT MACHINES:	SET 1		SET 2		SET 3		SET 4		SET 5		SET 6	
	WT.	REPS.	WT.	REPS.	WT.	REPS.	WT.	REPS.	WT.	REPS.	WT.	REPS.

MUSCLE GROUPS WORKED TODAY: ☐ ARMS ☐ CHEST ☐ BACK ☐ LEGS ☐ CORE ☐ OTHER

MY MOOD TODAY: **TO DO/NOTES:**

☐   ☐   ☐

WEIGHT:

WORKOUT LOG BOOK

DATE:	START:	FINISH:

☐ S ☐ M ☐ T ☐ W ☐ T ☐ F ☐ S   ☐ AM ☐ PM   ☐ AM ☐ PM

WORKOUT TYPE:	TIME/DISTANCE:	WATER(B OZ GLASSES)	VITAMINS/SUPPLEMENTS	
			DOSAGE	QTY.
☐ TREADMILL				
☐ ELLIPTICAL				
☐ BIKE				
☐ STAIR CLIMBER				
☐ OTHER				
☐ OTHER				

TIME/DISTANCE: **TIME/DISTANCE:**

☐ RUNNING/JOG					
☐ WALKING					
☐ BIKING					
☐ SWIMMING					
☐ YOGA					
☐ PILATES					
☐ OTHER					
☐ OTHER					

STRENGTH TRAINING

FREE WEIGHTS/ WEIGHT MACHINES:	SET 1		SET 2		SET 3		SET 4		SET 5		SET 6	
	WT.	REPS.	WT.	REPS.	WT.	REPS.	WT.	REPS.	WT.	REPS.	WT.	REPS.

MUSCLE GROUPS WORKED TODAY: ☐ ARMS ☐ CHEST ☐ BACK ☐ LEGS ☐ CORE ☐ OTHER

MY MOOD TODAY:	TO DO/NOTES:
☐ ☐ ☐	

WEIGHT:	

WORKOUT LOG BOOK

DATE:	START:	FINISH:

☐ S ☐ M ☐ T ☐ W ☐ T ☐ F ☐ S ☐ AM ☐ PM ☐ AM ☐ PM

WORKOUT TYPE:	TIME/DISTANCE:	WATER(B OZ GLASSES)	VITAMINS/SUPPLEMENTS	
			DOSAGE	QTY.
☐ TREADMILL				
☐ ELLIPTICAL				
☐ BIKE				
☐ STAIR CLIMBER				
☐ OTHER				
☐ OTHER				

TIME/DISTANCE: **TIME/DISTANCE:**

☐ RUNNING/JOG				
☐ WALKING				
☐ BIKING				
☐ SWIMMING				
☐ YOGA				
☐ PILATES				
☐ OTHER				
☐ OTHER				

STRENGTH TRAINING

FREE WEIGHTS/ WEIGHT MACHINES:	SET 1		SET 2		SET 3		SET 4		SET 5		SET 6	
	WT.	REPS.	WT.	REPS.	WT.	REPS.	WT.	REPS.	WT.	REPS.	WT.	REPS.

MUSCLE GROUPS WORKED TODAY: ☐ ARMS ☐ CHEST ☐ BACK ☐ LEGS ☐ CORE ☐ OTHER

MY MOOD TODAY:	TO DO/NOTES:
☐ ☐ ☐	

WEIGHT:

WORKOUT LOG BOOK

<table>
<tr><td>DATE:</td><td>START:</td><td>FINISH:</td></tr>
</table>

☐S ☐M ☐T ☐W ☐T ☐F ☐S   ☐AM ☐PM   ☐AM ☐PM

WORKOUT TYPE:	TIME/DISTANCE:	WATER(B OZ GLASSES)	VITAMINS/SUPPLEMENTS	
			DOSAGE	QTY.
☐ TREADMILL				
☐ ELLIPTICAL				
☐ BIKE				
☐ STAIR CLIMBER				
☐ OTHER				
☐ OTHER				

TIME/DISTANCE:

TIME/DISTANCE:

☐ RUNNING/JOG					
☐ WALKING					
☐ BIKING					
☐ SWIMMING					
☐ YOGA					
☐ PILATES					
☐ OTHER					
☐ OTHER					

STRENGTH TRAINING

FREE WEIGHTS/ WEIGHT MACHINES:	SET 1		SET 2		SET 3		SET 4		SET 5		SET 6	
	WT.	REPS.	WT.	REPS.	WT.	REPS.	WT.	REPS.	WT.	REPS.	WT.	REPS.

MUSCLE GROUPS WORKED TODAY: ☐ARMS ☐CHEST ☐BACK ☐LEGS ☐CORE ☐OTHER

MY MOOD TODAY:

☐   ☐   ☐

TO DO/NOTES:

WEIGHT:

WORKOUT LOG BOOK

DATE:	START:	FINISH:

☐S ☐M ☐T ☐W ☐T ☐F ☐S   ☐AM   ☐PM   ☐AM   ☐PM

WORKOUT TYPE:	TIME/DISTANCE:	WATER(B OZ GLASSES)	VITAMINS/SUPPLEMENTS	
			DOSAGE	QTY.
☐ TREADMILL				
☐ ELLIPTICAL				
☐ BIKE				
☐ STAIR CLIMBER				
☐ OTHER				
☐ OTHER				

TIME/DISTANCE: **TIME/DISTANCE:**

☐ RUNNING/JOG	
☐ WALKING	
☐ BIKING	
☐ SWIMMING	
☐ YOGA	
☐ PILATES	
☐ OTHER	
☐ OTHER	

STRENGTH TRAINING

FREE WEIGHTS/ WEIGHT MACHINES:	SET 1		SET 2		SET 3		SET 4		SET 5		SET 6	
	WT.	REPS.	WT.	REPS.	WT.	REPS.	WT.	REPS.	WT.	REPS.	WT.	REPS.

MUSCLE GROUPS WORKED TODAY: ☐ARMS ☐CHEST ☐BACK ☐LEGS ☐CORE ☐OTHER

MY MOOD TODAY:	TO DO/NOTES:
☹ ☐ 😐 ☐ 🙂 ☐	

WEIGHT:

WORKOUT LOG BOOK

DATE:	START:	FINISH:

☐ S ☐ M ☐ T ☐ W ☐ T ☐ F ☐ S   ☐ AM   ☐ PM   ☐ AM   ☐ PM

WORKOUT TYPE:	TIME/DISTANCE:	WATER(B OZ GLASSES)	VITAMINS/SUPPLEMENTS		
				DOSAGE	QTY.
☐ TREADMILL					
☐ ELLIPTICAL					
☐ BIKE					
☐ STAIR CLIMBER					
☐ OTHER					
☐ OTHER					

TIME/DISTANCE:

TIME/DISTANCE:

☐ RUNNING/JOG					
☐ WALKING					
☐ BIKING					
☐ SWIMMING					
☐ YOGA					
☐ PILATES					
☐ OTHER					
☐ OTHER					

STRENGTH TRAINING

FREE WEIGHTS/ WEIGHT MACHINES:	SET 1		SET 2		SET 3		SET 4		SET 5		SET 6	
	WT.	REPS.	WT.	REPS.	WT.	REPS.	WT.	REPS.	WT.	REPS.	WT.	REPS.

MUSCLE GROUPS WORKED TODAY: ☐ ARMS ☐ CHEST ☐ BACK ☐ LEGS ☐ CORE ☐ OTHER

MY MOOD TODAY:	TO DO/NOTES:
☹ ☐ 😐 ☐ 🙂 ☐	

WEIGHT:

WORKOUT LOG BOOK

DATE:	START:	FINISH:

☐ S ☐ M ☐ T ☐ W ☐ T ☐ F ☐ S   ☐ AM   ☐ PM   ☐ AM   ☐ PM

WORKOUT TYPE:	TIME/DISTANCE:	WATER(B OZ GLASSES)	VITAMINS/SUPPLEMENTS		
				DOSAGE	QTY.
☐ TREADMILL					
☐ ELLIPTICAL					
☐ BIKE					
☐ STAIR CLIMBER					
☐ OTHER					
☐ OTHER					

TIME/DISTANCE:	TIME/DISTANCE:			
☐ RUNNING/JOG				
☐ WALKING				
☐ BIKING				
☐ SWIMMING				
☐ YOGA				
☐ PILATES				
☐ OTHER				
☐ OTHER				

STRENGTH TRAINING

FREE WEIGHTS/ WEIGHT MACHINES:	SET 1		SET 2		SET 3		SET 4		SET 5		SET 6	
	WT.	REPS.	WT.	REPS.	WT.	REPS.	WT.	REPS.	WT.	REPS.	WT.	REPS.

MUSCLE GROUPS WORKED TODAY: ☐ ARMS ☐ CHEST ☐ BACK ☐ LEGS ☐ CORE ☐ OTHER

MY MOOD TODAY:	TO DO/NOTES:
☹ ☐ 😐 ☐ ☺ ☐	

WEIGHT:

WORKOUT LOG BOOK

DATE:	START:	FINISH:

☐ S ☐ M ☐ T ☐ W ☐ T ☐ F ☐ S   ☐ AM   ☐ PM   ☐ AM   ☐ PM

WORKOUT TYPE:	TIME/DISTANCE:	WATER(B OZ GLASSES)	VITAMINS/SUPPLEMENTS	
			DOSAGE	QTY.
☐ TREADMILL				
☐ ELLIPTICAL				
☐ BIKE				
☐ STAIR CLIMBER				
☐ OTHER				
☐ OTHER				

TIME/DISTANCE:

TIME/DISTANCE:

☐ RUNNING/JOG				
☐ WALKING				
☐ BIKING				
☐ SWIMMING				
☐ YOGA				
☐ PILATES				
☐ OTHER				
☐ OTHER				

STRENGTH TRAINING

FREE WEIGHTS/ WEIGHT MACHINES:	SET 1		SET 2		SET 3		SET 4		SET 5		SET 6	
	WT.	REPS.	WT.	REPS.	WT.	REPS.	WT.	REPS.	WT.	REPS.	WT.	REPS.

MUSCLE GROUPS WORKED TODAY: ☐ ARMS ☐ CHEST ☐ BACK ☐ LEGS ☐ CORE ☐ OTHER

MY MOOD TODAY:	TO DO/NOTES:
☹ ☐ 😐 ☐ 🙂 ☐	

WEIGHT:

WORKOUT LOG BOOK

DATE:	START:	FINISH:

☐S ☐M ☐T ☐W ☐T ☐F ☐S   ☐AM   ☐PM   ☐AM   ☐PM

WORKOUT TYPE:	TIME/DISTANCE:	WATER(B OZ GLASSES)	VITAMINS/SUPPLEMENTS	
			DOSAGE	QTY.
☐ TREADMILL				
☐ ELLIPTICAL				
☐ BIKE				
☐ STAIR CLIMBER				
☐ OTHER				
☐ OTHER				

TIME/DISTANCE: **TIME/DISTANCE:**

☐ RUNNING/JOG					
☐ WALKING					
☐ BIKING					
☐ SWIMMING					
☐ YOGA					
☐ PILATES					
☐ OTHER					
☐ OTHER					

STRENGTH TRAINING

FREE WEIGHTS/ WEIGHT MACHINES:	SET 1		SET 2		SET 3		SET 4		SET 5		SET 6	
	WT.	REPS.	WT.	REPS.	WT.	REPS.	WT.	REPS.	WT.	REPS.	WT.	REPS.

MUSCLE GROUPS WORKED TODAY: ☐ARMS ☐CHEST ☐BACK ☐LEGS ☐CORE ☐OTHER

MY MOOD TODAY:	TO DO/NOTES:
☐ ☐ ☐	

WEIGHT:

WORKOUT LOG BOOK

DATE:	START:	FINISH:

☐ S ☐ M ☐ T ☐ W ☐ T ☐ F ☐ S   ☐ AM   ☐ PM   ☐ AM   ☐ PM

WORKOUT TYPE:	TIME/DISTANCE:	WATER(B OZ GLASSES)	VITAMINS/SUPPLEMENTS

WATER(B OZ GLASSES)

VITAMINS/SUPPLEMENTS

	DOSAGE	QTY.

WORKOUT TYPE:
- ☐ TREADMILL
- ☐ ELLIPTICAL
- ☐ BIKE
- ☐ STAIR CLIMBER
- ☐ OTHER
- ☐ OTHER

TIME/DISTANCE:
- ☐ RUNNING/JOG
- ☐ WALKING
- ☐ BIKING
- ☐ SWIMMING
- ☐ YOGA
- ☐ PILATES
- ☐ OTHER
- ☐ OTHER

TIME/DISTANCE:

STRENGTH TRAINING

FREE WEIGHTS/ WEIGHT MACHINES:	SET 1		SET 2		SET 3		SET 4		SET 5		SET 6	
	WT.	REPS.	WT.	REPS.	WT.	REPS.	WT.	REPS.	WT.	REPS.	WT.	REPS.

MUSCLE GROUPS WORKED TODAY: ☐ ARMS ☐ CHEST ☐ BACK ☐ LEGS ☐ CORE ☐ OTHER

MY MOOD TODAY:	TO DO/NOTES:
☹ ☐ 😐 ☐ 🙂 ☐	

WEIGHT:

WORKOUT LOG BOOK

DATE:	START:	FINISH:

☐S ☐M ☐T ☐W ☐T ☐F ☐S   ☐AM ☐PM   ☐AM ☐PM

WORKOUT TYPE:	TIME/DISTANCE:	WATER(B OZ GLASSES)	VITAMINS/SUPPLEMENTS	
			DOSAGE	QTY.
☐ TREADMILL				
☐ ELLIPTICAL				
☐ BIKE				
☐ STAIR CLIMBER				
☐ OTHER				
☐ OTHER				

TIME/DISTANCE:

TIME/DISTANCE:

☐ RUNNING/JOG					
☐ WALKING					
☐ BIKING					
☐ SWIMMING					
☐ YOGA					
☐ PILATES					
☐ OTHER					
☐ OTHER					

STRENGTH TRAINING

FREE WEIGHTS/ WEIGHT MACHINES:	SET 1		SET 2		SET 3		SET 4		SET 5		SET 6	
	WT.	REPS.	WT.	REPS.	WT.	REPS.	WT.	REPS.	WT.	REPS.	WT.	REPS.

MUSCLE GROUPS WORKED TODAY: ☐ARMS ☐CHEST ☐BACK ☐LEGS ☐CORE ☐OTHER

MY MOOD TODAY:

TO DO/NOTES:

☐   ☐   ☐

WEIGHT:

WORKOUT LOG BOOK

DATE:	START:	FINISH:

☐ S ☐ M ☐ T ☐ W ☐ T ☐ F ☐ S   ☐ AM   ☐ PM   ☐ AM   ☐ PM

WORKOUT TYPE:	TIME/DISTANCE:	WATER(B OZ GLASSES)	VITAMINS/SUPPLEMENTS	
			DOSAGE	QTY.
☐ TREADMILL				
☐ ELLIPTICAL				
☐ BIKE				
☐ STAIR CLIMBER				
☐ OTHER				
☐ OTHER				

TIME/DISTANCE: **TIME/DISTANCE:**

☐ RUNNING/JOG					
☐ WALKING					
☐ BIKING					
☐ SWIMMING					
☐ YOGA					
☐ PILATES					
☐ OTHER					
☐ OTHER					

STRENGTH TRAINING

FREE WEIGHTS/ WEIGHT MACHINES:	SET 1		SET 2		SET 3		SET 4		SET 5		SET 6	
	WT.	REPS.	WT.	REPS.	WT.	REPS.	WT.	REPS.	WT.	REPS.	WT.	REPS.

MUSCLE GROUPS WORKED TODAY: ☐ ARMS ☐ CHEST ☐ BACK ☐ LEGS ☐ CORE ☐ OTHER

MY MOOD TODAY: **TO DO/NOTES:**

☐   ☐   ☐

WEIGHT:

WORKOUT LOG BOOK

DATE:	START:	FINISH:

☐ S ☐ M ☐ T ☐ W ☐ T ☐ F ☐ S   ☐ AM   ☐ PM   ☐ AM   ☐ PM

WORKOUT TYPE:	TIME/DISTANCE:	WATER(B OZ GLASSES)	VITAMINS/SUPPLEMENTS	
			DOSAGE	QTY.
☐ TREADMILL				
☐ ELLIPTICAL				
☐ BIKE				
☐ STAIR CLIMBER				
☐ OTHER				
☐ OTHER				

TIME/DISTANCE:		TIME/DISTANCE:			
☐ RUNNING/JOG					
☐ WALKING					
☐ BIKING					
☐ SWIMMING					
☐ YOGA					
☐ PILATES					
☐ OTHER					
☐ OTHER					

STRENGTH TRAINING

FREE WEIGHTS/ WEIGHT MACHINES:	SET 1		SET 2		SET 3		SET 4		SET 5		SET 6	
	WT.	REPS.	WT.	REPS.	WT.	REPS.	WT.	REPS.	WT.	REPS.	WT.	REPS.

MUSCLE GROUPS WORKED TODAY: ☐ ARMS ☐ CHEST ☐ BACK ☐ LEGS ☐ CORE ☐ OTHER

MY MOOD TODAY:	TO DO/NOTES:
☐ ☐ ☐	

WEIGHT:

WORKOUT LOG BOOK

DATE:	START:	FINISH:

☐ S ☐ M ☐ T ☐ W ☐ T ☐ F ☐ S   ☐ AM ☐ PM   ☐ AM ☐ PM

WORKOUT TYPE:	TIME/DISTANCE:	WATER(B OZ GLASSES)	VITAMINS/SUPPLEMENTS	
			DOSAGE	QTY.
☐ TREADMILL				
☐ ELLIPTICAL				
☐ BIKE				
☐ STAIR CLIMBER				
☐ OTHER				
☐ OTHER				

TIME/DISTANCE:

TIME/DISTANCE:

☐ RUNNING/JOG						
☐ WALKING						
☐ BIKING						
☐ SWIMMING						
☐ YOGA						
☐ PILATES						
☐ OTHER						
☐ OTHER						

STRENGTH TRAINING

FREE WEIGHTS/ WEIGHT MACHINES:	SET 1		SET 2		SET 3		SET 4		SET 5		SET 6	
	WT.	REPS.	WT.	REPS.	WT.	REPS.	WT.	REPS.	WT.	REPS.	WT.	REPS.

MUSCLE GROUPS WORKED TODAY: ☐ ARMS ☐ CHEST ☐ BACK ☐ LEGS ☐ CORE ☐ OTHER

MY MOOD TODAY:	TO DO/NOTES:
☐ ☐ ☐	

WEIGHT:

WORKOUT LOG BOOK

DATE:	START:	FINISH:

☐S ☐M ☐T ☐W ☐T ☐F ☐S   ☐AM   ☐PM   ☐AM   ☐PM

WORKOUT TYPE:	TIME/DISTANCE:	WATER(B OZ GLASSES)	VITAMINS/SUPPLEMENTS	
			DOSAGE	QTY.
☐ TREADMILL				
☐ ELLIPTICAL				
☐ BIKE				
☐ STAIR CLIMBER				
☐ OTHER				
☐ OTHER				

TIME/DISTANCE: TIME/DISTANCE:

☐ RUNNING/JOG				
☐ WALKING				
☐ BIKING				
☐ SWIMMING				
☐ YOGA				
☐ PILATES				
☐ OTHER				
☐ OTHER				

STRENGTH TRAINING

FREE WEIGHTS/ WEIGHT MACHINES:	SET 1		SET 2		SET 3		SET 4		SET 5		SET 6	
	WT.	REPS.	WT.	REPS.	WT.	REPS.	WT.	REPS.	WT.	REPS.	WT.	REPS.

MUSCLE GROUPS WORKED TODAY: ☐ARMS ☐CHEST ☐BACK ☐LEGS ☐CORE ☐OTHER

MY MOOD TODAY:

TO DO/NOTES:

☹ ☐   😐 ☐   🙂 ☐

WEIGHT:

WORKOUT LOG BOOK

DATE:	START:	FINISH:

☐ S ☐ M ☐ T ☐ W ☐ T ☐ F ☐ S   ☐ AM   ☐ PM   ☐ AM   ☐ PM

WORKOUT TYPE:	TIME/DISTANCE:	WATER(B OZ GLASSES)	VITAMINS/SUPPLEMENTS	
			DOSAGE	QTY.
☐ TREADMILL				
☐ ELLIPTICAL				
☐ BIKE				
☐ STAIR CLIMBER				
☐ OTHER				
☐ OTHER				

TIME/DISTANCE: **TIME/DISTANCE:**

☐ RUNNING/JOG					
☐ WALKING					
☐ BIKING					
☐ SWIMMING					
☐ YOGA					
☐ PILATES					
☐ OTHER					
☐ OTHER					

STRENGTH TRAINING

FREE WEIGHTS/ WEIGHT MACHINES:	SET 1		SET 2		SET 3		SET 4		SET 5		SET 6	
	WT.	REPS.	WT.	REPS.	WT.	REPS.	WT.	REPS.	WT.	REPS.	WT.	REPS.

MUSCLE GROUPS WORKED TODAY: ☐ ARMS ☐ CHEST ☐ BACK ☐ LEGS ☐ CORE ☐ OTHER

MY MOOD TODAY:	TO DO/NOTES:
☹ ☐ 😐 ☐ ☺ ☐	

WEIGHT:

WORKOUT LOG BOOK

DATE:	START:	FINISH:

☐S ☐M ☐T ☐W ☐T ☐F ☐S   ☐AM ☐PM   ☐AM ☐PM

WORKOUT TYPE:	TIME/DISTANCE:	WATER(B OZ GLASSES)	VITAMINS/SUPPLEMENTS		
				DOSAGE	QTY.
☐ TREADMILL					
☐ ELLIPTICAL					
☐ BIKE					
☐ STAIR CLIMBER					
☐ OTHER					
☐ OTHER					

TIME/DISTANCE: **TIME/DISTANCE:**

☐ RUNNING/JOG					
☐ WALKING					
☐ BIKING					
☐ SWIMMING					
☐ YOGA					
☐ PILATES					
☐ OTHER					
☐ OTHER					

STRENGTH TRAINING

FREE WEIGHTS/ WEIGHT MACHINES:	SET 1		SET 2		SET 3		SET 4		SET 5		SET 6	
	WT.	REPS.	WT.	REPS.	WT.	REPS.	WT.	REPS.	WT.	REPS.	WT.	REPS.

MUSCLE GROUPS WORKED TODAY: ☐ARMS ☐CHEST ☐BACK ☐LEGS ☐CORE ☐OTHER

MY MOOD TODAY:	TO DO/NOTES:
☹ ☐ 😐 ☐ 🙂 ☐	

WEIGHT:

WORKOUT LOG BOOK

DATE:	START:	FINISH:

☐ S ☐ M ☐ T ☐ W ☐ T ☐ F ☐ S   ☐ AM   ☐ PM   ☐ AM   ☐ PM

WORKOUT TYPE:	TIME/DISTANCE:	WATER(B OZ GLASSES)	VITAMINS/SUPPLEMENTS	
			DOSAGE	QTY.
☐ TREADMILL				
☐ ELLIPTICAL				
☐ BIKE				
☐ STAIR CLIMBER				
☐ OTHER				
☐ OTHER				

TIME/DISTANCE: **TIME/DISTANCE:**

☐ RUNNING/JOG	
☐ WALKING	
☐ BIKING	
☐ SWIMMING	
☐ YOGA	
☐ PILATES	
☐ OTHER	
☐ OTHER	

STRENGTH TRAINING

FREE WEIGHTS/ WEIGHT MACHINES:	SET 1		SET 2		SET 3		SET 4		SET 5		SET 6	
	WT.	REPS.	WT.	REPS.	WT.	REPS.	WT.	REPS.	WT.	REPS.	WT.	REPS.

MUSCLE GROUPS WORKED TODAY: ☐ ARMS ☐ CHEST ☐ BACK ☐ LEGS ☐ CORE ☐ OTHER

MY MOOD TODAY: **TO DO/NOTES:**

☐   ☐   ☐

WEIGHT:

WORKOUT LOG BOOK

DATE:	START:	FINISH:

☐ S ☐ M ☐ T ☐ W ☐ T ☐ F ☐ S   ☐ AM   ☐ PM   ☐ AM   ☐ PM

WORKOUT TYPE:	TIME/DISTANCE:	WATER(B OZ GLASSES)	VITAMINS/SUPPLEMENTS		
				DOSAGE	QTY.
☐ TREADMILL					
☐ ELLIPTICAL					
☐ BIKE					
☐ STAIR CLIMBER					
☐ OTHER					
☐ OTHER					

TIME/DISTANCE: **TIME/DISTANCE:**

TIME/DISTANCE:		TIME/DISTANCE:				
☐ RUNNING/JOG						
☐ WALKING						
☐ BIKING						
☐ SWIMMING						
☐ YOGA						
☐ PILATES						
☐ OTHER						
☐ OTHER						

STRENGTH TRAINING

FREE WEIGHTS/ WEIGHT MACHINES:	SET 1		SET 2		SET 3		SET 4		SET 5		SET 6	
	WT.	REPS.	WT.	REPS.	WT.	REPS.	WT.	REPS.	WT.	REPS.	WT.	REPS.

MUSCLE GROUPS WORKED TODAY: ☐ ARMS ☐ CHEST ☐ BACK ☐ LEGS ☐ CORE ☐ OTHER

MY MOOD TODAY: **TO DO/NOTES:**

☐   ☐   ☐

WEIGHT:

WORKOUT LOG BOOK

DATE:	START:	FINISH:

☐ S ☐ M ☐ T ☐ W ☐ T ☐ F ☐ S   ☐ AM ☐ PM   ☐ AM ☐ PM

WORKOUT TYPE:	TIME/DISTANCE:	WATER(B OZ GLASSES)	VITAMINS/SUPPLEMENTS		
				DOSAGE	QTY.
☐ TREADMILL					
☐ ELLIPTICAL					
☐ BIKE					
☐ STAIR CLIMBER					
☐ OTHER					
☐ OTHER					

TIME/DISTANCE: **TIME/DISTANCE:**

TIME/DISTANCE:						
☐ RUNNING/JOG						
☐ WALKING						
☐ BIKING						
☐ SWIMMING						
☐ YOGA						
☐ PILATES						
☐ OTHER						
☐ OTHER						

STRENGTH TRAINING

FREE WEIGHTS/ WEIGHT MACHINES:	SET 1		SET 2		SET 3		SET 4		SET 5		SET 6	
	WT.	REPS.	WT.	REPS.	WT.	REPS.	WT.	REPS.	WT.	REPS.	WT.	REPS.

MUSCLE GROUPS WORKED TODAY: ☐ ARMS ☐ CHEST ☐ BACK ☐ LEGS ☐ CORE ☐ OTHER

MY MOOD TODAY:	TO DO/NOTES:

WEIGHT:

WORKOUT LOG BOOK

DATE:	START:	FINISH:

☐ S ☐ M ☐ T ☐ W ☐ T ☐ F ☐ S   ☐ AM   ☐ PM   ☐ AM   ☐ PM

WORKOUT TYPE:	TIME/DISTANCE:	WATER(B OZ GLASSES)	VITAMINS/SUPPLEMENTS	
			DOSAGE	QTY.
☐ TREADMILL				
☐ ELLIPTICAL				
☐ BIKE				
☐ STAIR CLIMBER				
☐ OTHER				
☐ OTHER				

TIME/DISTANCE: **TIME/DISTANCE:**

☐ RUNNING/JOG					
☐ WALKING					
☐ BIKING					
☐ SWIMMING					
☐ YOGA					
☐ PILATES					
☐ OTHER					
☐ OTHER					

STRENGTH TRAINING

FREE WEIGHTS/ WEIGHT MACHINES:	SET 1		SET 2		SET 3		SET 4		SET 5		SET 6	
	WT.	REPS.	WT.	REPS.	WT.	REPS.	WT.	REPS.	WT.	REPS.	WT.	REPS.

MUSCLE GROUPS WORKED TODAY: ☐ ARMS ☐ CHEST ☐ BACK ☐ LEGS ☐ CORE ☐ OTHER

MY MOOD TODAY:	TO DO/NOTES:
☹ ☐ 😐 ☐ 🙂 ☐	

WEIGHT:	

WORKOUT LOG BOOK

DATE:	START:	FINISH:

☐ S ☐ M ☐ T ☐ W ☐ T ☐ F ☐ S   ☐ AM   ☐ PM   ☐ AM   ☐ PM

WORKOUT TYPE:	TIME/DISTANCE:	WATER(B OZ GLASSES)	VITAMINS/SUPPLEMENTS	
			DOSAGE	QTY.
☐ TREADMILL				
☐ ELLIPTICAL				
☐ BIKE				
☐ STAIR CLIMBER				
☐ OTHER				
☐ OTHER				

TIME/DISTANCE:

TIME/DISTANCE:

☐ RUNNING/JOG					
☐ WALKING					
☐ BIKING					
☐ SWIMMING					
☐ YOGA					
☐ PILATES					
☐ OTHER					
☐ OTHER					

STRENGTH TRAINING

FREE WEIGHTS/ WEIGHT MACHINES:	SET 1		SET 2		SET 3		SET 4		SET 5		SET 6	
	WT.	REPS.	WT.	REPS.	WT.	REPS.	WT.	REPS.	WT.	REPS.	WT.	REPS.

MUSCLE GROUPS WORKED TODAY: ☐ ARMS ☐ CHEST ☐ BACK ☐ LEGS ☐ CORE ☐ OTHER

MY MOOD TODAY:	TO DO/NOTES:
☹ ☐ 😐 ☐ 🙂 ☐	

WEIGHT:

WORKOUT LOG BOOK

DATE:	START:	FINISH:

☐ S ☐ M ☐ T ☐ W ☐ T ☐ F ☐ S   ☐ AM   ☐ PM   ☐ AM   ☐ PM

WORKOUT TYPE:	TIME/DISTANCE:	WATER(B OZ GLASSES)	VITAMINS/SUPPLEMENTS	
			DOSAGE	QTY.
☐ TREADMILL				
☐ ELLIPTICAL				
☐ BIKE				
☐ STAIR CLIMBER				
☐ OTHER				
☐ OTHER				

TIME/DISTANCE: **TIME/DISTANCE:**

☐ RUNNING/JOG					
☐ WALKING					
☐ BIKING					
☐ SWIMMING					
☐ YOGA					
☐ PILATES					
☐ OTHER					
☐ OTHER					

STRENGTH TRAINING

FREE WEIGHTS/ WEIGHT MACHINES:	SET 1		SET 2		SET 3		SET 4		SET 5		SET 6	
	WT.	REPS.	WT.	REPS.	WT.	REPS.	WT.	REPS.	WT.	REPS.	WT.	REPS.

MUSCLE GROUPS WORKED TODAY: ☐ ARMS ☐ CHEST ☐ BACK ☐ LEGS ☐ CORE ☐ OTHER

MY MOOD TODAY:	TO DO/NOTES:
☹ ☐ 😐 ☐ ☺ ☐	

WEIGHT:

WORKOUT LOG BOOK

DATE:	START:	FINISH:

☐ S ☐ M ☐ T ☐ W ☐ T ☐ F ☐ S   ☐ AM   ☐ PM   ☐ AM   ☐ PM

WORKOUT TYPE:	TIME/DISTANCE:	WATER(B OZ GLASSES)	VITAMINS/SUPPLEMENTS	
			DOSAGE	QTY.
☐ TREADMILL				
☐ ELLIPTICAL				
☐ BIKE				
☐ STAIR CLIMBER				
☐ OTHER				
☐ OTHER				

TIME/DISTANCE:		TIME/DISTANCE:			
☐ RUNNING/JOG					
☐ WALKING					
☐ BIKING					
☐ SWIMMING					
☐ YOGA					
☐ PILATES					
☐ OTHER					
☐ OTHER					

STRENGTH TRAINING

FREE WEIGHTS/ WEIGHT MACHINES:	SET 1		SET 2		SET 3		SET 4		SET 5		SET 6	
	WT.	REPS.	WT.	REPS.	WT.	REPS.	WT.	REPS.	WT.	REPS.	WT.	REPS.

MUSCLE GROUPS WORKED TODAY: ☐ ARMS ☐ CHEST ☐ BACK ☐ LEGS ☐ CORE ☐ OTHER

MY MOOD TODAY:	TO DO/NOTES:
☐ ☐ ☐	

WEIGHT:

WORKOUT LOG BOOK

DATE:	START:	FINISH:

☐S ☐M ☐T ☐W ☐T ☐F ☐S　　　☐AM　☐PM　　　☐AM　☐PM

WORKOUT TYPE:	TIME/DISTANCE:	WATER(B OZ GLASSES)	VITAMINS/SUPPLEMENTS	
			DOSAGE	QTY.
☐ TREADMILL				
☐ ELLIPTICAL				
☐ BIKE				
☐ STAIR CLIMBER				
☐ OTHER				
☐ OTHER				

TIME/DISTANCE:　　　　　　**TIME/DISTANCE:**

☐ RUNNING/JOG		
☐ WALKING		
☐ BIKING		
☐ SWIMMING		
☐ YOGA		
☐ PILATES		
☐ OTHER		
☐ OTHER		

STRENGTH TRAINING

FREE WEIGHTS/ WEIGHT MACHINES:	SET 1		SET 2		SET 3		SET 4		SET 5		SET 6	
	WT.	REPS.	WT.	REPS.	WT.	REPS.	WT.	REPS.	WT.	REPS.	WT.	REPS.

MUSCLE GROUPS WORKED TODAY:　☐ARMS ☐CHEST ☐BACK ☐LEGS ☐CORE ☐OTHER

MY MOOD TODAY:　　　　　　**TO DO/NOTES:**

☐　　☐　　☐

WEIGHT:

WORKOUT LOG BOOK

DATE:	START:	FINISH:

☐ S ☐ M ☐ T ☐ W ☐ T ☐ F ☐ S   ☐ AM ☐ PM   ☐ AM ☐ PM

WORKOUT TYPE:	TIME/DISTANCE:	WATER(B OZ GLASSES)	VITAMINS/SUPPLEMENTS	
			DOSAGE	QTY.
☐ TREADMILL				
☐ ELLIPTICAL				
☐ BIKE				
☐ STAIR CLIMBER				
☐ OTHER				
☐ OTHER				

TIME/DISTANCE: **TIME/DISTANCE:**

- ☐ RUNNING/JOG
- ☐ WALKING
- ☐ BIKING
- ☐ SWIMMING
- ☐ YOGA
- ☐ PILATES
- ☐ OTHER
- ☐ OTHER

STRENGTH TRAINING

FREE WEIGHTS/ WEIGHT MACHINES:	SET 1		SET 2		SET 3		SET 4		SET 5		SET 6	
	WT.	REPS.	WT.	REPS.	WT.	REPS.	WT.	REPS.	WT.	REPS.	WT.	REPS.

MUSCLE GROUPS WORKED TODAY: ☐ ARMS ☐ CHEST ☐ BACK ☐ LEGS ☐ CORE ☐ OTHER

MY MOOD TODAY: TO DO/NOTES:

☐   ☐   ☐

WEIGHT:

WORKOUT LOG BOOK

DATE:	START:	FINISH:

☐ S ☐ M ☐ T ☐ W ☐ T ☐ F ☐ S   ☐ AM   ☐ PM   ☐ AM   ☐ PM

WORKOUT TYPE:	TIME/DISTANCE:	WATER(B OZ GLASSES)	VITAMINS/SUPPLEMENTS	
			DOSAGE	QTY.
☐ TREADMILL				
☐ ELLIPTICAL				
☐ BIKE				
☐ STAIR CLIMBER				
☐ OTHER				
☐ OTHER				

TIME/DISTANCE: **TIME/DISTANCE:**

☐ RUNNING/JOG					
☐ WALKING					
☐ BIKING					
☐ SWIMMING					
☐ YOGA					
☐ PILATES					
☐ OTHER					
☐ OTHER					

STRENGTH TRAINING

FREE WEIGHTS/ WEIGHT MACHINES:	SET 1		SET 2		SET 3		SET 4		SET 5		SET 6	
	WT.	REPS.	WT.	REPS.	WT.	REPS.	WT.	REPS.	WT.	REPS.	WT.	REPS.

MUSCLE GROUPS WORKED TODAY: ☐ ARMS ☐ CHEST ☐ BACK ☐ LEGS ☐ CORE ☐ OTHER

MY MOOD TODAY: **TO DO/NOTES:**

☐   ☐   ☐

WEIGHT:

WORKOUT LOG BOOK

DATE:	START:	FINISH:

☐ S ☐ M ☐ T ☐ W ☐ T ☐ F ☐ S   ☐ AM   ☐ PM   ☐ AM   ☐ PM

WORKOUT TYPE:	TIME/DISTANCE:	WATER(8 OZ GLASSES)	VITAMINS/SUPPLEMENTS	
			DOSAGE	QTY.
☐ TREADMILL				
☐ ELLIPTICAL				
☐ BIKE				
☐ STAIR CLIMBER				
☐ OTHER				
☐ OTHER				

TIME/DISTANCE: **TIME/DISTANCE:**

RUNNING/JOG	WALKING	BIKING	SWIMMING	YOGA	PILATES	OTHER	OTHER

- ☐ RUNNING/JOG
- ☐ WALKING
- ☐ BIKING
- ☐ SWIMMING
- ☐ YOGA
- ☐ PILATES
- ☐ OTHER
- ☐ OTHER

STRENGTH TRAINING

FREE WEIGHTS/ WEIGHT MACHINES:	SET 1		SET 2		SET 3		SET 4		SET 5		SET 6	
	WT.	REPS.	WT.	REPS.	WT.	REPS.	WT.	REPS.	WT.	REPS.	WT.	REPS.

MUSCLE GROUPS WORKED TODAY: ☐ ARMS ☐ CHEST ☐ BACK ☐ LEGS ☐ CORE ☐ OTHER

MY MOOD TODAY:	TO DO/NOTES:

☐   ☐   ☐

WEIGHT:

WORKOUT LOG BOOK

DATE:	START:	FINISH:

☐S ☐M ☐T ☐W ☐T ☐F ☐S   ☐AM ☐PM   ☐AM ☐PM

WORKOUT TYPE:	TIME/DISTANCE:	WATER(B OZ GLASSES)	VITAMINS/SUPPLEMENTS	
			DOSAGE	QTY.
☐ TREADMILL				
☐ ELLIPTICAL				
☐ BIKE				
☐ STAIR CLIMBER				
☐ OTHER				
☐ OTHER				

TIME/DISTANCE: **TIME/DISTANCE:**

☐ RUNNING/JOG					
☐ WALKING					
☐ BIKING					
☐ SWIMMING					
☐ YOGA					
☐ PILATES					
☐ OTHER					
☐ OTHER					

STRENGTH TRAINING

FREE WEIGHTS/ WEIGHT MACHINES:	SET 1		SET 2		SET 3		SET 4		SET 5		SET 6	
	WT.	REPS.	WT.	REPS.	WT.	REPS.	WT.	REPS.	WT.	REPS.	WT.	REPS.

MUSCLE GROUPS WORKED TODAY: ☐ARMS ☐CHEST ☐BACK ☐LEGS ☐CORE ☐OTHER

MY MOOD TODAY: **TO DO/NOTES:**

☐ ☐ ☐

WEIGHT:

WORKOUT LOG BOOK

DATE:	START:	FINISH:

☐ S ☐ M ☐ T ☐ W ☐ T ☐ F ☐ S   ☐ AM ☐ PM   ☐ AM ☐ PM

WORKOUT TYPE:	TIME/DISTANCE:	WATER(B OZ GLASSES)	VITAMINS/SUPPLEMENTS	
			DOSAGE	QTY.
☐ TREADMILL				
☐ ELLIPTICAL				
☐ BIKE				
☐ STAIR CLIMBER				
☐ OTHER				
☐ OTHER				

TIME/DISTANCE:		TIME/DISTANCE:		
☐ RUNNING/JOG				
☐ WALKING				
☐ BIKING				
☐ SWIMMING				
☐ YOGA				
☐ PILATES				
☐ OTHER				
☐ OTHER				

STRENGTH TRAINING

FREE WEIGHTS/ WEIGHT MACHINES:	SET 1		SET 2		SET 3		SET 4		SET 5		SET 6	
	WT.	REPS.	WT.	REPS.	WT.	REPS.	WT.	REPS.	WT.	REPS.	WT.	REPS.

MUSCLE GROUPS WORKED TODAY: ☐ ARMS ☐ CHEST ☐ BACK ☐ LEGS ☐ CORE ☐ OTHER

MY MOOD TODAY:	TO DO/NOTES:
☹ ☐ ☺ ☐ ☺ ☐	

WEIGHT:

WORKOUT LOG BOOK

DATE:	START:	FINISH:

☐ S ☐ M ☐ T ☐ W ☐ T ☐ F ☐ S   ☐ AM   ☐ PM   ☐ AM   ☐ PM

WORKOUT TYPE:	TIME/DISTANCE:	WATER(B OZ GLASSES)	VITAMINS/SUPPLEMENTS	
			DOSAGE	QTY.
☐ TREADMILL				
☐ ELLIPTICAL				
☐ BIKE				
☐ STAIR CLIMBER				
☐ OTHER				
☐ OTHER				

TIME/DISTANCE:

TIME/DISTANCE:

| RUNNING/JOG | WALKING | BIKING | SWIMMING | YOGA | PILATES | OTHER | OTHER |

- ☐ RUNNING/JOG
- ☐ WALKING
- ☐ BIKING
- ☐ SWIMMING
- ☐ YOGA
- ☐ PILATES
- ☐ OTHER
- ☐ OTHER

STRENGTH TRAINING

FREE WEIGHTS/ WEIGHT MACHINES:	SET 1		SET 2		SET 3		SET 4		SET 5		SET 6	
	WT.	REPS.	WT.	REPS.	WT.	REPS.	WT.	REPS.	WT.	REPS.	WT.	REPS.

MUSCLE GROUPS WORKED TODAY: ☐ ARMS ☐ CHEST ☐ BACK ☐ LEGS ☐ CORE ☐ OTHER

MY MOOD TODAY: **TO DO/NOTES:**

☐   ☐   ☐

WEIGHT:

WORKOUT LOG BOOK

DATE:	START:	FINISH:

☐ S ☐ M ☐ T ☐ W ☐ T ☐ F ☐ S   ☐ AM   ☐ PM   ☐ AM   ☐ PM

WORKOUT TYPE:	TIME/DISTANCE:	WATER(B OZ GLASSES)	VITAMINS/SUPPLEMENTS	
			DOSAGE	QTY.
☐ TREADMILL				
☐ ELLIPTICAL				
☐ BIKE				
☐ STAIR CLIMBER				
☐ OTHER				
☐ OTHER				

TIME/DISTANCE:

TIME/DISTANCE:

☐ RUNNING/JOG					
☐ WALKING					
☐ BIKING					
☐ SWIMMING					
☐ YOGA					
☐ PILATES					
☐ OTHER					
☐ OTHER					

STRENGTH TRAINING

FREE WEIGHTS/ WEIGHT MACHINES:	SET 1		SET 2		SET 3		SET 4		SET 5		SET 6	
	WT.	REPS.	WT.	REPS.	WT.	REPS.	WT.	REPS.	WT.	REPS.	WT.	REPS.

MUSCLE GROUPS WORKED TODAY: ☐ ARMS ☐ CHEST ☐ BACK ☐ LEGS ☐ CORE ☐ OTHER

MY MOOD TODAY:	TO DO/NOTES:
☹ ☐ 😐 ☐ 🙂 ☐	

WEIGHT:

WORKOUT LOG BOOK

DATE:	START:	FINISH:

☐S ☐M ☐T ☐W ☐T ☐F ☐S   ☐AM ☐PM   ☐AM ☐PM

WORKOUT TYPE:	TIME/DISTANCE:	WATER(B OZ GLASSES)	VITAMINS/SUPPLEMENTS	
			DOSAGE	QTY.
☐ TREADMILL				
☐ ELLIPTICAL				
☐ BIKE				
☐ STAIR CLIMBER				
☐ OTHER				
☐ OTHER				

TIME/DISTANCE: **TIME/DISTANCE:**

☐ RUNNING/JOG					
☐ WALKING					
☐ BIKING					
☐ SWIMMING					
☐ YOGA					
☐ PILATES					
☐ OTHER					
☐ OTHER					

STRENGTH TRAINING

FREE WEIGHTS/ WEIGHT MACHINES:	SET 1		SET 2		SET 3		SET 4		SET 5		SET 6	
	WT.	REPS.	WT.	REPS.	WT.	REPS.	WT.	REPS.	WT.	REPS.	WT.	REPS.

MUSCLE GROUPS WORKED TODAY: ☐ARMS ☐CHEST ☐BACK ☐LEGS ☐CORE ☐OTHER

MY MOOD TODAY:	TO DO/NOTES:
☺ ☺ ☺ ☐ ☐ ☐	

WEIGHT:

WORKOUT LOG BOOK

DATE:	START:	FINISH:

☐ S ☐ M ☐ T ☐ W ☐ T ☐ F ☐ S   ☐ AM   ☐ PM   ☐ AM   ☐ PM

WORKOUT TYPE:	TIME/DISTANCE:	WATER(B OZ GLASSES)	VITAMINS/SUPPLEMENTS		
				DOSAGE	QTY.
☐ TREADMILL					
☐ ELLIPTICAL					
☐ BIKE					
☐ STAIR CLIMBER					
☐ OTHER					
☐ OTHER					

TIME/DISTANCE: **TIME/DISTANCE:**

☐ RUNNING/JOG					
☐ WALKING					
☐ BIKING					
☐ SWIMMING					
☐ YOGA					
☐ PILATES					
☐ OTHER					
☐ OTHER					

STRENGTH TRAINING

FREE WEIGHTS/ WEIGHT MACHINES:	SET 1		SET 2		SET 3		SET 4		SET 5		SET 6	
	WT.	REPS.	WT.	REPS.	WT.	REPS.	WT.	REPS.	WT.	REPS.	WT.	REPS.

MUSCLE GROUPS WORKED TODAY: ☐ ARMS ☐ CHEST ☐ BACK ☐ LEGS ☐ CORE ☐ OTHER

MY MOOD TODAY:	TO DO/NOTES:
☹ 😐 🙂	
☐ ☐ ☐	

WEIGHT:	

WORKOUT LOG BOOK

DATE:	START:	FINISH:

☐ S ☐ M ☐ T ☐ W ☐ T ☐ F ☐ S   ☐ AM   ☐ PM   ☐ AM   ☐ PM

WORKOUT TYPE:	TIME/DISTANCE:	WATER(B OZ GLASSES)	VITAMINS/SUPPLEMENTS	
			DOSAGE	QTY.
☐ TREADMILL				
☐ ELLIPTICAL				
☐ BIKE				
☐ STAIR CLIMBER				
☐ OTHER				
☐ OTHER				

TIME/DISTANCE: **TIME/DISTANCE:**

☐ RUNNING/JOG					
☐ WALKING					
☐ BIKING					
☐ SWIMMING					
☐ YOGA					
☐ PILATES					
☐ OTHER					
☐ OTHER					

STRENGTH TRAINING

FREE WEIGHTS/ WEIGHT MACHINES:	SET 1		SET 2		SET 3		SET 4		SET 5		SET 6	
	WT.	REPS.	WT.	REPS.	WT.	REPS.	WT.	REPS.	WT.	REPS.	WT.	REPS.

MUSCLE GROUPS WORKED TODAY: ☐ ARMS ☐ CHEST ☐ BACK ☐ LEGS ☐ CORE ☐ OTHER

MY MOOD TODAY:	TO DO/NOTES:
☹ 😐 ☺ ☐ ☐ ☐	

WEIGHT:

WORKOUT LOG BOOK

DATE:	START:	FINISH:

☐ S ☐ M ☐ T ☐ W ☐ T ☐ F ☐ S   ☐ AM   ☐ PM   ☐ AM   ☐ PM

WORKOUT TYPE:	TIME/DISTANCE:	WATER(B OZ GLASSES)	VITAMINS/SUPPLEMENTS	
			DOSAGE	QTY.
☐ TREADMILL				
☐ ELLIPTICAL				
☐ BIKE				
☐ STAIR CLIMBER				
☐ OTHER				
☐ OTHER				

TIME/DISTANCE: **TIME/DISTANCE:**

Activity					
☐ RUNNING/JOG					
☐ WALKING					
☐ BIKING					
☐ SWIMMING					
☐ YOGA					
☐ PILATES					
☐ OTHER					
☐ OTHER					

STRENGTH TRAINING

FREE WEIGHTS/ WEIGHT MACHINES:	SET 1		SET 2		SET 3		SET 4		SET 5		SET 6	
	WT.	REPS.	WT.	REPS.	WT.	REPS.	WT.	REPS.	WT.	REPS.	WT.	REPS.

MUSCLE GROUPS WORKED TODAY: ☐ ARMS ☐ CHEST ☐ BACK ☐ LEGS ☐ CORE ☐ OTHER

MY MOOD TODAY:	TO DO/NOTES:
☹ ☐ 😐 ☐ 🙂 ☐	

WEIGHT:

WORKOUT LOG BOOK

DATE:	START:	FINISH:

☐ S ☐ M ☐ T ☐ W ☐ T ☐ F ☐ S ☐ AM ☐ PM ☐ AM ☐ PM

WORKOUT TYPE:	TIME/DISTANCE:	WATER(B OZ GLASSES)	VITAMINS/SUPPLEMENTS	
			DOSAGE	QTY.
☐ TREADMILL				
☐ ELLIPTICAL				
☐ BIKE				
☐ STAIR CLIMBER				
☐ OTHER				
☐ OTHER				

TIME/DISTANCE:		TIME/DISTANCE:			
☐ RUNNING/JOG					
☐ WALKING					
☐ BIKING					
☐ SWIMMING					
☐ YOGA					
☐ PILATES					
☐ OTHER					
☐ OTHER					

STRENGTH TRAINING

FREE WEIGHTS/ WEIGHT MACHINES:	SET 1		SET 2		SET 3		SET 4		SET 5		SET 6	
	WT.	REPS.	WT.	REPS.	WT.	REPS.	WT.	REPS.	WT.	REPS.	WT.	REPS.

MUSCLE GROUPS WORKED TODAY: ☐ ARMS ☐ CHEST ☐ BACK ☐ LEGS ☐ CORE ☐ OTHER

MY MOOD TODAY:	TO DO/NOTES:
☹ ☐ ☐ ☺ ☐	

WEIGHT:

WORKOUT LOG BOOK

DATE:	START:	FINISH:

☐ S ☐ M ☐ T ☐ W ☐ T ☐ F ☐ S ☐ AM ☐ PM ☐ AM ☐ PM

WORKOUT TYPE:	TIME/DISTANCE:	WATER(B OZ GLASSES)	VITAMINS/SUPPLEMENTS		
				DOSAGE	QTY.
☐ TREADMILL					
☐ ELLIPTICAL					
☐ BIKE					
☐ STAIR CLIMBER					
☐ OTHER					
☐ OTHER					

TIME/DISTANCE:

TIME/DISTANCE:

☐ RUNNING/JOG				
☐ WALKING				
☐ BIKING				
☐ SWIMMING				
☐ YOGA				
☐ PILATES				
☐ OTHER				
☐ OTHER				

STRENGTH TRAINING

FREE WEIGHTS/ WEIGHT MACHINES:	SET 1		SET 2		SET 3		SET 4		SET 5		SET 6	
	WT.	REPS.	WT.	REPS.	WT.	REPS.	WT.	REPS.	WT.	REPS.	WT.	REPS.

MUSCLE GROUPS WORKED TODAY: ☐ ARMS ☐ CHEST ☐ BACK ☐ LEGS ☐ CORE ☐ OTHER

MY MOOD TODAY:

TO DO/NOTES:

☐   ☐   ☐

WEIGHT:

WORKOUT LOG BOOK

DATE:	START:	FINISH:

☐ S ☐ M ☐ T ☐ W ☐ T ☐ F ☐ S   ☐ AM   ☐ PM   ☐ AM   ☐ PM

WORKOUT TYPE:	TIME/DISTANCE:	WATER(B OZ GLASSES)	VITAMINS/SUPPLEMENTS	
			DOSAGE	QTY.
☐ TREADMILL				
☐ ELLIPTICAL				
☐ BIKE				
☐ STAIR CLIMBER				
☐ OTHER				
☐ OTHER				

TIME/DISTANCE: **TIME/DISTANCE:**

☐ RUNNING/JOG						
☐ WALKING						
☐ BIKING						
☐ SWIMMING						
☐ YOGA						
☐ PILATES						
☐ OTHER						
☐ OTHER						

STRENGTH TRAINING

FREE WEIGHTS/ WEIGHT MACHINES:	SET 1		SET 2		SET 3		SET 4		SET 5		SET 6	
	WT.	REPS.	WT.	REPS.	WT.	REPS.	WT.	REPS.	WT.	REPS.	WT.	REPS.

MUSCLE GROUPS WORKED TODAY: ☐ ARMS ☐ CHEST ☐ BACK ☐ LEGS ☐ CORE ☐ OTHER

MY MOOD TODAY:	TO DO/NOTES:
☹ ☐ 😐 ☐ 🙂 ☐	

WEIGHT:

WORKOUT LOG BOOK

DATE:	START:	FINISH:

☐ S ☐ M ☐ T ☐ W ☐ T ☐ F ☐ S   ☐ AM   ☐ PM   ☐ AM   ☐ PM

WORKOUT TYPE:	TIME/DISTANCE:	WATER(B OZ GLASSES)	VITAMINS/SUPPLEMENTS	
			DOSAGE	QTY.
☐ TREADMILL				
☐ ELLIPTICAL				
☐ BIKE				
☐ STAIR CLIMBER				
☐ OTHER				
☐ OTHER				

TIME/DISTANCE: **TIME/DISTANCE:**

☐ RUNNING/JOG					
☐ WALKING					
☐ BIKING					
☐ SWIMMING					
☐ YOGA					
☐ PILATES					
☐ OTHER					
☐ OTHER					

STRENGTH TRAINING

FREE WEIGHTS/ WEIGHT MACHINES:	SET 1		SET 2		SET 3		SET 4		SET 5		SET 6	
	WT.	REPS.	WT.	REPS.	WT.	REPS.	WT.	REPS.	WT.	REPS.	WT.	REPS.

MUSCLE GROUPS WORKED TODAY: ☐ ARMS ☐ CHEST ☐ BACK ☐ LEGS ☐ CORE ☐ OTHER

MY MOOD TODAY:	TO DO/NOTES:
☹ ☐ 😐 ☐ 🙂 ☐	

WEIGHT:

WORKOUT LOG BOOK

DATE:	START:	FINISH:

☐ S ☐ M ☐ T ☐ W ☐ T ☐ F ☐ S   ☐ AM ☐ PM   ☐ AM ☐ PM

WORKOUT TYPE:	TIME/DISTANCE:	WATER(B OZ GLASSES)	VITAMINS/SUPPLEMENTS	
			DOSAGE	QTY.
☐ TREADMILL				
☐ ELLIPTICAL				
☐ BIKE				
☐ STAIR CLIMBER				
☐ OTHER				
☐ OTHER				

TIME/DISTANCE: **TIME/DISTANCE:**

☐ RUNNING/JOG					
☐ WALKING					
☐ BIKING					
☐ SWIMMING					
☐ YOGA					
☐ PILATES					
☐ OTHER					
☐ OTHER					

STRENGTH TRAINING

FREE WEIGHTS/ WEIGHT MACHINES:	SET 1		SET 2		SET 3		SET 4		SET 5		SET 6	
	WT.	REPS.	WT.	REPS.	WT.	REPS.	WT.	REPS.	WT.	REPS.	WT.	REPS.

MUSCLE GROUPS WORKED TODAY: ☐ ARMS ☐ CHEST ☐ BACK ☐ LEGS ☐ CORE ☐ OTHER

MY MOOD TODAY:	TO DO/NOTES:
☹ ☐ 😐 ☐ ☺ ☐	

WEIGHT:

WORKOUT LOG BOOK

DATE:	START:	FINISH:

☐ S ☐ M ☐ T ☐ W ☐ T ☐ F ☐ S   ☐ AM   ☐ PM   ☐ AM   ☐ PM

WORKOUT TYPE:	TIME/DISTANCE:	WATER(B OZ GLASSES)	VITAMINS/SUPPLEMENTS		
				DOSAGE	QTY.
☐ TREADMILL					
☐ ELLIPTICAL					
☐ BIKE					
☐ STAIR CLIMBER					
☐ OTHER					
☐ OTHER					

TIME/DISTANCE: **TIME/DISTANCE:**

RUNNING/JOG etc.					
☐ RUNNING/JOG					
☐ WALKING					
☐ BIKING					
☐ SWIMMING					
☐ YOGA					
☐ PILATES					
☐ OTHER					
☐ OTHER					

STRENGTH TRAINING

FREE WEIGHTS/ WEIGHT MACHINES:	SET 1		SET 2		SET 3		SET 4		SET 5		SET 6	
	WT.	REPS.	WT.	REPS.	WT.	REPS.	WT.	REPS.	WT.	REPS.	WT.	REPS.

MUSCLE GROUPS WORKED TODAY: ☐ ARMS ☐ CHEST ☐ BACK ☐ LEGS ☐ CORE ☐ OTHER

MY MOOD TODAY:	TO DO/NOTES:
☹ ☐ 😐 ☐ 🙂 ☐	

WEIGHT:

WORKOUT LOG BOOK

DATE:	START:	FINISH:

☐ S ☐ M ☐ T ☐ W ☐ T ☐ F ☐ S   ☐ AM   ☐ PM   ☐ AM   ☐ PM

WORKOUT TYPE:	TIME/DISTANCE:	WATER(B OZ GLASSES)	VITAMINS/SUPPLEMENTS		
				DOSAGE	QTY.
☐ TREADMILL					
☐ ELLIPTICAL					
☐ BIKE					
☐ STAIR CLIMBER					
☐ OTHER					
☐ OTHER					

TIME/DISTANCE: **TIME/DISTANCE:**

☐ RUNNING/JOG					
☐ WALKING					
☐ BIKING					
☐ SWIMMING					
☐ YOGA					
☐ PILATES					
☐ OTHER					
☐ OTHER					

STRENGTH TRAINING

FREE WEIGHTS/ WEIGHT MACHINES:	SET 1		SET 2		SET 3		SET 4		SET 5		SET 6	
	WT.	REPS.	WT.	REPS.	WT.	REPS.	WT.	REPS.	WT.	REPS.	WT.	REPS.

MUSCLE GROUPS WORKED TODAY: ☐ ARMS ☐ CHEST ☐ BACK ☐ LEGS ☐ CORE ☐ OTHER

MY MOOD TODAY:	TO DO/NOTES:
☹ ☐ 😐 ☐ ☺ ☐	

WEIGHT:

WORKOUT LOG BOOK

DATE:	START:	FINISH:

☐S ☐M ☐T ☐W ☐T ☐F ☐S   ☐AM   ☐PM   ☐AM   ☐PM

WORKOUT TYPE:	TIME/DISTANCE:	WATER(B OZ GLASSES)	VITAMINS/SUPPLEMENTS		
☐ TREADMILL				DOSAGE	QTY.
☐ ELLIPTICAL					
☐ BIKE					
☐ STAIR CLIMBER					
☐ OTHER					
☐ OTHER					

TIME/DISTANCE: **TIME/DISTANCE:**

☐ RUNNING/JOG	
☐ WALKING	
☐ BIKING	
☐ SWIMMING	
☐ YOGA	
☐ PILATES	
☐ OTHER	
☐ OTHER	

STRENGTH TRAINING

FREE WEIGHTS/ WEIGHT MACHINES:	SET 1		SET 2		SET 3		SET 4		SET 5		SET 6	
	WT.	REPS.	WT.	REPS.	WT.	REPS.	WT.	REPS.	WT.	REPS.	WT.	REPS.

MUSCLE GROUPS WORKED TODAY: ☐ARMS ☐CHEST ☐BACK ☐LEGS ☐CORE ☐OTHER

MY MOOD TODAY:	TO DO/NOTES:
☹ ☐ 😐 ☐ 🙂 ☐	

WEIGHT:

WORKOUT LOG BOOK

DATE:	START:	FINISH:

☐S ☐M ☐T ☐W ☐T ☐F ☐S   ☐AM ☐PM   ☐AM ☐PM

WORKOUT TYPE:	TIME/DISTANCE:	WATER(B OZ GLASSES)	VITAMINS/SUPPLEMENTS	
			DOSAGE	QTY.
☐ TREADMILL				
☐ ELLIPTICAL				
☐ BIKE				
☐ STAIR CLIMBER				
☐ OTHER				
☐ OTHER				

TIME/DISTANCE: **TIME/DISTANCE:**

RUNNING/JOG	WALKING	BIKING	SWIMMING	YOGA	PILATES	OTHER	OTHER
☐	☐	☐	☐	☐	☐	☐	☐

STRENGTH TRAINING

FREE WEIGHTS/ WEIGHT MACHINES:	SET 1		SET 2		SET 3		SET 4		SET 5		SET 6	
	WT.	REPS.	WT.	REPS.	WT.	REPS.	WT.	REPS.	WT.	REPS.	WT.	REPS.

MUSCLE GROUPS WORKED TODAY: ☐ARMS ☐CHEST ☐BACK ☐LEGS ☐CORE ☐OTHER

MY MOOD TODAY:	TO DO/NOTES:
☐ ☐ ☐	

WEIGHT:	

WORKOUT LOG BOOK

DATE:	START:	FINISH:

☐S ☐M ☐T ☐W ☐T ☐F ☐S   ☐AM   ☐PM   ☐AM   ☐PM

WORKOUT TYPE:	TIME/DISTANCE:	WATER(B OZ GLASSES)	VITAMINS/SUPPLEMENTS	
			DOSAGE	QTY.
☐ TREADMILL				
☐ ELLIPTICAL				
☐ BIKE				
☐ STAIR CLIMBER				
☐ OTHER				
☐ OTHER				

TIME/DISTANCE: **TIME/DISTANCE:**

☐ RUNNING/JOG						
☐ WALKING						
☐ BIKING						
☐ SWIMMING						
☐ YOGA						
☐ PILATES						
☐ OTHER						
☐ OTHER						

STRENGTH TRAINING

FREE WEIGHTS/ WEIGHT MACHINES:	SET 1		SET 2		SET 3		SET 4		SET 5		SET 6	
	WT.	REPS.	WT.	REPS.	WT.	REPS.	WT.	REPS.	WT.	REPS.	WT.	REPS.

MUSCLE GROUPS WORKED TODAY: ☐ARMS ☐CHEST ☐BACK ☐LEGS ☐CORE ☐OTHER

MY MOOD TODAY:	TO DO/NOTES:
☐ ☐ ☐	

WEIGHT:

WORKOUT LOG BOOK

DATE:	START:	FINISH:

☐ S ☐ M ☐ T ☐ W ☐ T ☐ F ☐ S   ☐ AM   ☐ PM   ☐ AM   ☐ PM

WORKOUT TYPE:	TIME/DISTANCE:	WATER(B OZ GLASSES)	VITAMINS/SUPPLEMENTS	
			DOSAGE	QTY.
☐ TREADMILL				
☐ ELLIPTICAL				
☐ BIKE				
☐ STAIR CLIMBER				
☐ OTHER				
☐ OTHER				

TIME/DISTANCE: **TIME/DISTANCE:**

☐ RUNNING/JOG					
☐ WALKING					
☐ BIKING					
☐ SWIMMING					
☐ YOGA					
☐ PILATES					
☐ OTHER					
☐ OTHER					

STRENGTH TRAINING

FREE WEIGHTS/ WEIGHT MACHINES:	SET 1		SET 2		SET 3		SET 4		SET 5		SET 6	
	WT.	REPS.	WT.	REPS.	WT.	REPS.	WT.	REPS.	WT.	REPS.	WT.	REPS.

MUSCLE GROUPS WORKED TODAY: ☐ ARMS ☐ CHEST ☐ BACK ☐ LEGS ☐ CORE ☐ OTHER

MY MOOD TODAY: **TO DO/NOTES:**

☹ ☐   😐 ☐   🙂 ☐

WEIGHT:

WORKOUT LOG BOOK

DATE:	START:	FINISH:

☐ S ☐ M ☐ T ☐ W ☐ T ☐ F ☐ S   ☐ AM   ☐ PM   ☐ AM   ☐ PM

WORKOUT TYPE:	TIME/DISTANCE:	WATER (8 OZ GLASSES)	VITAMINS/SUPPLEMENTS	
			DOSAGE	QTY.
☐ TREADMILL				
☐ ELLIPTICAL				
☐ BIKE				
☐ STAIR CLIMBER				
☐ OTHER				
☐ OTHER				

TIME/DISTANCE:

	TIME/DISTANCE:				
☐ RUNNING/JOG					
☐ WALKING					
☐ BIKING					
☐ SWIMMING					
☐ YOGA					
☐ PILATES					
☐ OTHER					
☐ OTHER					

STRENGTH TRAINING

FREE WEIGHTS/ WEIGHT MACHINES:	SET 1		SET 2		SET 3		SET 4		SET 5		SET 6	
	WT.	REPS.	WT.	REPS.	WT.	REPS.	WT.	REPS.	WT.	REPS.	WT.	REPS.

MUSCLE GROUPS WORKED TODAY: ☐ ARMS ☐ CHEST ☐ BACK ☐ LEGS ☐ CORE ☐ OTHER

MY MOOD TODAY:	TO DO/NOTES:
☐ ☐ ☐	

WEIGHT:

WORKOUT LOG BOOK

DATE:	START:	FINISH:

☐ S ☐ M ☐ T ☐ W ☐ T ☐ F ☐ S   ☐ AM   ☐ PM   ☐ AM   ☐ PM

WORKOUT TYPE:	TIME/DISTANCE:	WATER(B OZ GLASSES)	VITAMINS/SUPPLEMENTS		
				DOSAGE	QTY.
☐ TREADMILL					
☐ ELLIPTICAL					
☐ BIKE					
☐ STAIR CLIMBER					
☐ OTHER					
☐ OTHER					

TIME/DISTANCE: **TIME/DISTANCE:**

☐ RUNNING/JOG					
☐ WALKING					
☐ BIKING					
☐ SWIMMING					
☐ YOGA					
☐ PILATES					
☐ OTHER					
☐ OTHER					

STRENGTH TRAINING

FREE WEIGHTS/ WEIGHT MACHINES:	SET 1		SET 2		SET 3		SET 4		SET 5		SET 6	
	WT.	REPS.	WT.	REPS.	WT.	REPS.	WT.	REPS.	WT.	REPS.	WT.	REPS.

MUSCLE GROUPS WORKED TODAY: ☐ ARMS ☐ CHEST ☐ BACK ☐ LEGS ☐ CORE ☐ OTHER

MY MOOD TODAY: TO DO/NOTES:

☐   ☐   ☐

WEIGHT:

WORKOUT LOG BOOK

DATE:	START:	FINISH:

☐ S ☐ M ☐ T ☐ W ☐ T ☐ F ☐ S   ☐ AM   ☐ PM   ☐ AM   ☐ PM

WORKOUT TYPE:	TIME/DISTANCE:	WATER(B OZ GLASSES)	VITAMINS/SUPPLEMENTS	
			DOSAGE	QTY.
☐ TREADMILL				
☐ ELLIPTICAL				
☐ BIKE				
☐ STAIR CLIMBER				
☐ OTHER				
☐ OTHER				

TIME/DISTANCE: **TIME/DISTANCE:**

☐ RUNNING/JOG					
☐ WALKING					
☐ BIKING					
☐ SWIMMING					
☐ YOGA					
☐ PILATES					
☐ OTHER					
☐ OTHER					

STRENGTH TRAINING

FREE WEIGHTS/ WEIGHT MACHINES:	SET 1		SET 2		SET 3		SET 4		SET 5		SET 6	
	WT.	REPS.	WT.	REPS.	WT.	REPS.	WT.	REPS.	WT.	REPS.	WT.	REPS.

MUSCLE GROUPS WORKED TODAY: ☐ ARMS ☐ CHEST ☐ BACK ☐ LEGS ☐ CORE ☐ OTHER

MY MOOD TODAY:	TO DO/NOTES:
☹ ☐ 😐 ☐ 🙂 ☐	

WEIGHT:

WORKOUT LOG BOOK

DATE:	START:	FINISH:

☐ S ☐ M ☐ T ☐ W ☐ T ☐ F ☐ S   ☐ AM   ☐ PM   ☐ AM   ☐ PM

WORKOUT TYPE:	TIME/DISTANCE:	WATER(B OZ GLASSES)	VITAMINS/SUPPLEMENTS	
			DOSAGE	QTY.
☐ TREADMILL				
☐ ELLIPTICAL				
☐ BIKE				
☐ STAIR CLIMBER				
☐ OTHER				
☐ OTHER				

TIME/DISTANCE: **TIME/DISTANCE:**

RUNNING/JOG		
☐ RUNNING/JOG		
☐ WALKING		
☐ BIKING		
☐ SWIMMING		
☐ YOGA		
☐ PILATES		
☐ OTHER		
☐ OTHER		

STRENGTH TRAINING

FREE WEIGHTS/ WEIGHT MACHINES:	SET 1		SET 2		SET 3		SET 4		SET 5		SET 6	
	WT.	REPS.	WT.	REPS.	WT.	REPS.	WT.	REPS.	WT.	REPS.	WT.	REPS.

MUSCLE GROUPS WORKED TODAY: ☐ ARMS ☐ CHEST ☐ BACK ☐ LEGS ☐ CORE ☐ OTHER

MY MOOD TODAY:	TO DO/NOTES:
☹ ☐ 😐 ☐ 🙂 ☐	

WEIGHT:

WORKOUT LOG BOOK

DATE:	START:	FINISH:

☐ S ☐ M ☐ T ☐ W ☐ T ☐ F ☐ S   ☐ AM   ☐ PM   ☐ AM   ☐ PM

WORKOUT TYPE:	TIME/DISTANCE:	WATER(B OZ GLASSES)	VITAMINS/SUPPLEMENTS	
			DOSAGE	QTY.
☐ TREADMILL				
☐ ELLIPTICAL				
☐ BIKE				
☐ STAIR CLIMBER				
☐ OTHER				
☐ OTHER				

TIME/DISTANCE:		TIME/DISTANCE:			
☐ RUNNING/JOG					
☐ WALKING					
☐ BIKING					
☐ SWIMMING					
☐ YOGA					
☐ PILATES					
☐ OTHER					
☐ OTHER					

STRENGTH TRAINING

FREE WEIGHTS/ WEIGHT MACHINES:	SET 1		SET 2		SET 3		SET 4		SET 5		SET 6	
	WT.	REPS.	WT.	REPS.	WT.	REPS.	WT.	REPS.	WT.	REPS.	WT.	REPS.

MUSCLE GROUPS WORKED TODAY: ☐ ARMS ☐ CHEST ☐ BACK ☐ LEGS ☐ CORE ☐ OTHER

MY MOOD TODAY:

TO DO/NOTES:

☐ ☐ ☐

WEIGHT:

WORKOUT LOG BOOK

DATE:	START:	FINISH:

☐ S ☐ M ☐ T ☐ W ☐ T ☐ F ☐ S   ☐ AM ☐ PM   ☐ AM ☐ PM

WORKOUT TYPE:	TIME/DISTANCE:	WATER(B OZ GLASSES)	VITAMINS/SUPPLEMENTS	
			DOSAGE	QTY.
☐ TREADMILL				
☐ ELLIPTICAL				
☐ BIKE				
☐ STAIR CLIMBER				
☐ OTHER				
☐ OTHER				

TIME/DISTANCE: **TIME/DISTANCE:**

☐ RUNNING/JOG					
☐ WALKING					
☐ BIKING					
☐ SWIMMING					
☐ YOGA					
☐ PILATES					
☐ OTHER					
☐ OTHER					

STRENGTH TRAINING

FREE WEIGHTS/ WEIGHT MACHINES:	SET 1		SET 2		SET 3		SET 4		SET 5		SET 6	
	WT.	REPS.	WT.	REPS.	WT.	REPS.	WT.	REPS.	WT.	REPS.	WT.	REPS.

MUSCLE GROUPS WORKED TODAY: ☐ ARMS ☐ CHEST ☐ BACK ☐ LEGS ☐ CORE ☐ OTHER

MY MOOD TODAY: **TO DO/NOTES:**

☐   ☐   ☐

WEIGHT:

WORKOUT LOG BOOK

DATE:	START:	FINISH:

☐ S ☐ M ☐ T ☐ W ☐ T ☐ F ☐ S   ☐ AM   ☐ PM   ☐ AM   ☐ PM

WORKOUT TYPE:	TIME/DISTANCE:	WATER(B OZ GLASSES)	VITAMINS/SUPPLEMENTS		
				DOSAGE	QTY.
☐ TREADMILL					
☐ ELLIPTICAL					
☐ BIKE					
☐ STAIR CLIMBER					
☐ OTHER					
☐ OTHER					

TIME/DISTANCE: **TIME/DISTANCE:**

☐ RUNNING/JOG					
☐ WALKING					
☐ BIKING					
☐ SWIMMING					
☐ YOGA					
☐ PILATES					
☐ OTHER					
☐ OTHER					

STRENGTH TRAINING

FREE WEIGHTS/ WEIGHT MACHINES:	SET 1		SET 2		SET 3		SET 4		SET 5		SET 6	
	WT.	REPS.	WT.	REPS.	WT.	REPS.	WT.	REPS.	WT.	REPS.	WT.	REPS.

MUSCLE GROUPS WORKED TODAY: ☐ ARMS ☐ CHEST ☐ BACK ☐ LEGS ☐ CORE ☐ OTHER

MY MOOD TODAY:	TO DO/NOTES:
☐ ☐ ☐	

WEIGHT:

WORKOUT LOG BOOK

DATE:	START:	FINISH:

☐ S ☐ M ☐ T ☐ W ☐ T ☐ F ☐ S   ☐ AM   ☐ PM   ☐ AM   ☐ PM

WORKOUT TYPE:	TIME/DISTANCE:	WATER(B OZ GLASSES)	VITAMINS/SUPPLEMENTS		
				DOSAGE	QTY.
☐ TREADMILL					
☐ ELLIPTICAL					
☐ BIKE					
☐ STAIR CLIMBER					
☐ OTHER					
☐ OTHER					

TIME/DISTANCE: **TIME/DISTANCE:**

☐ RUNNING/JOG					
☐ WALKING					
☐ BIKING					
☐ SWIMMING					
☐ YOGA					
☐ PILATES					
☐ OTHER					
☐ OTHER					

STRENGTH TRAINING

FREE WEIGHTS/ WEIGHT MACHINES:	SET 1		SET 2		SET 3		SET 4		SET 5		SET 6	
	WT.	REPS.	WT.	REPS.	WT.	REPS.	WT.	REPS.	WT.	REPS.	WT.	REPS.

MUSCLE GROUPS WORKED TODAY: ☐ ARMS ☐ CHEST ☐ BACK ☐ LEGS ☐ CORE ☐ OTHER

MY MOOD TODAY:	TO DO/NOTES:
☹ ☐ 😐 ☐ ☺ ☐	

WEIGHT:

WORKOUT LOG BOOK

DATE:	START:	FINISH:

☐ S ☐ M ☐ T ☐ W ☐ T ☐ F ☐ S   ☐ AM ☐ PM   ☐ AM ☐ PM

WORKOUT TYPE:	TIME/DISTANCE:	WATER(B OZ GLASSES)	VITAMINS/SUPPLEMENTS		
				DOSAGE	QTY.
☐ TREADMILL					
☐ ELLIPTICAL					
☐ BIKE					
☐ STAIR CLIMBER					
☐ OTHER					
☐ OTHER					

TIME/DISTANCE: **TIME/DISTANCE:**

☐ RUNNING/JOG					
☐ WALKING					
☐ BIKING					
☐ SWIMMING					
☐ YOGA					
☐ PILATES					
☐ OTHER					
☐ OTHER					

STRENGTH TRAINING

FREE WEIGHTS/ WEIGHT MACHINES:	SET 1		SET 2		SET 3		SET 4		SET 5		SET 6	
	WT.	REPS.	WT.	REPS.	WT.	REPS.	WT.	REPS.	WT.	REPS.	WT.	REPS.

MUSCLE GROUPS WORKED TODAY: ☐ ARMS ☐ CHEST ☐ BACK ☐ LEGS ☐ CORE ☐ OTHER

MY MOOD TODAY:	TO DO/NOTES:
☹ ☐ 😐 ☐ 🙂 ☐	

WEIGHT:

WORKOUT LOG BOOK

DATE:	START:	FINISH:

☐ S ☐ M ☐ T ☐ W ☐ T ☐ F ☐ S ☐ AM ☐ PM ☐ AM ☐ PM

WORKOUT TYPE:	TIME/DISTANCE:	WATER(B OZ GLASSES)	VITAMINS/SUPPLEMENTS		
				DOSAGE	QTY.
☐ TREADMILL					
☐ ELLIPTICAL					
☐ BIKE					
☐ STAIR CLIMBER					
☐ OTHER					
☐ OTHER					

TIME/DISTANCE: **TIME/DISTANCE:**

☐ RUNNING/JOG						
☐ WALKING						
☐ BIKING						
☐ SWIMMING						
☐ YOGA						
☐ PILATES						
☐ OTHER						
☐ OTHER						

STRENGTH TRAINING

FREE WEIGHTS/ WEIGHT MACHINES:	SET 1		SET 2		SET 3		SET 4		SET 5		SET 6	
	WT.	REPS.	WT.	REPS.	WT.	REPS.	WT.	REPS.	WT.	REPS.	WT.	REPS.

MUSCLE GROUPS WORKED TODAY: ☐ ARMS ☐ CHEST ☐ BACK ☐ LEGS ☐ CORE ☐ OTHER

MY MOOD TODAY:	TO DO/NOTES:
☹ ☐ 😐 ☐ 🙂 ☐	

WEIGHT:

WORKOUT LOG BOOK

DATE:	START:	FINISH:

☐ S ☐ M ☐ T ☐ W ☐ T ☐ F ☐ S   ☐ AM   ☐ PM   ☐ AM   ☐ PM

WORKOUT TYPE:	TIME/DISTANCE:	WATER(B OZ GLASSES)	VITAMINS/SUPPLEMENTS	
			DOSAGE	QTY.
☐ TREADMILL				
☐ ELLIPTICAL				
☐ BIKE				
☐ STAIR CLIMBER				
☐ OTHER				
☐ OTHER				

TIME/DISTANCE: **TIME/DISTANCE:**

☐ RUNNING/JOG	
☐ WALKING	
☐ BIKING	
☐ SWIMMING	
☐ YOGA	
☐ PILATES	
☐ OTHER	
☐ OTHER	

STRENGTH TRAINING

FREE WEIGHTS/ WEIGHT MACHINES:	SET 1		SET 2		SET 3		SET 4		SET 5		SET 6	
	WT.	REPS.	WT.	REPS.	WT.	REPS.	WT.	REPS.	WT.	REPS.	WT.	REPS.

MUSCLE GROUPS WORKED TODAY: ☐ ARMS ☐ CHEST ☐ BACK ☐ LEGS ☐ CORE ☐ OTHER

MY MOOD TODAY:	TO DO/NOTES:
☐ ☐ ☐	

WEIGHT:

WORKOUT LOG BOOK

DATE:	START:	FINISH:

☐ S ☐ M ☐ T ☐ W ☐ T ☐ F ☐ S   ☐ AM ☐ PM   ☐ AM ☐ PM

WORKOUT TYPE:	TIME/DISTANCE:	WATER(B OZ GLASSES)	VITAMINS/SUPPLEMENTS	
			DOSAGE	QTY.
☐ TREADMILL				
☐ ELLIPTICAL				
☐ BIKE				
☐ STAIR CLIMBER				
☐ OTHER				
☐ OTHER				

TIME/DISTANCE: **TIME/DISTANCE:**

☐ RUNNING/JOG						
☐ WALKING						
☐ BIKING						
☐ SWIMMING						
☐ YOGA						
☐ PILATES						
☐ OTHER						
☐ OTHER						

STRENGTH TRAINING

FREE WEIGHTS/ WEIGHT MACHINES:	SET 1		SET 2		SET 3		SET 4		SET 5		SET 6	
	WT.	REPS.	WT.	REPS.	WT.	REPS.	WT.	REPS.	WT.	REPS.	WT.	REPS.

MUSCLE GROUPS WORKED TODAY: ☐ ARMS ☐ CHEST ☐ BACK ☐ LEGS ☐ CORE ☐ OTHER

MY MOOD TODAY: **TO DO/NOTES:**

☐ ☐ ☐

WEIGHT:

WORKOUT LOG BOOK

DATE:	START:	FINISH:

☐ S ☐ M ☐ T ☐ W ☐ T ☐ F ☐ S   ☐ AM   ☐ PM   ☐ AM   ☐ PM

WORKOUT TYPE:	TIME/DISTANCE:	WATER(B OZ GLASSES)	VITAMINS/SUPPLEMENTS	
			DOSAGE	QTY.
☐ TREADMILL				
☐ ELLIPTICAL				
☐ BIKE				
☐ STAIR CLIMBER				
☐ OTHER				
☐ OTHER				

TIME/DISTANCE: **TIME/DISTANCE:**

☐ RUNNING/JOG					
☐ WALKING					
☐ BIKING					
☐ SWIMMING					
☐ YOGA					
☐ PILATES					
☐ OTHER					
☐ OTHER					

STRENGTH TRAINING

FREE WEIGHTS/ WEIGHT MACHINES:	SET 1		SET 2		SET 3		SET 4		SET 5		SET 6	
	WT.	REPS.	WT.	REPS.	WT.	REPS.	WT.	REPS.	WT.	REPS.	WT.	REPS.

MUSCLE GROUPS WORKED TODAY: ☐ ARMS ☐ CHEST ☐ BACK ☐ LEGS ☐ CORE ☐ OTHER

MY MOOD TODAY:	TO DO/NOTES:
☐ ☐ ☐	

WEIGHT:

WORKOUT LOG BOOK

DATE:	START:	FINISH:

☐ S ☐ M ☐ T ☐ W ☐ T ☐ F ☐ S   ☐ AM ☐ PM   ☐ AM ☐ PM

WORKOUT TYPE:	TIME/DISTANCE:	WATER(B OZ GLASSES)	VITAMINS/SUPPLEMENTS	
			DOSAGE	QTY.
☐ TREADMILL				
☐ ELLIPTICAL				
☐ BIKE				
☐ STAIR CLIMBER				
☐ OTHER				
☐ OTHER				

TIME/DISTANCE: **TIME/DISTANCE:**

☐ RUNNING/JOG					
☐ WALKING					
☐ BIKING					
☐ SWIMMING					
☐ YOGA					
☐ PILATES					
☐ OTHER					
☐ OTHER					

STRENGTH TRAINING

FREE WEIGHTS/ WEIGHT MACHINES:	SET 1		SET 2		SET 3		SET 4		SET 5		SET 6	
	WT.	REPS.	WT.	REPS.	WT.	REPS.	WT.	REPS.	WT.	REPS.	WT.	REPS.

MUSCLE GROUPS WORKED TODAY: ☐ ARMS ☐ CHEST ☐ BACK ☐ LEGS ☐ CORE ☐ OTHER

MY MOOD TODAY: **TO DO/NOTES:**

☐   ☐   ☐

WEIGHT:

WORKOUT LOG BOOK

DATE:	START:	FINISH:

☐ S ☐ M ☐ T ☐ W ☐ T ☐ F ☐ S   ☐ AM   ☐ PM   ☐ AM   ☐ PM

WORKOUT TYPE:	TIME/DISTANCE:	WATER(B OZ GLASSES)	VITAMINS/SUPPLEMENTS	
			DOSAGE	QTY.
☐ TREADMILL				
☐ ELLIPTICAL				
☐ BIKE				
☐ STAIR CLIMBER				
☐ OTHER				
☐ OTHER				

TIME/DISTANCE: **TIME/DISTANCE:**

☐ RUNNING/JOG					
☐ WALKING					
☐ BIKING					
☐ SWIMMING					
☐ YOGA					
☐ PILATES					
☐ OTHER					
☐ OTHER					

STRENGTH TRAINING

FREE WEIGHTS/ WEIGHT MACHINES:	SET 1		SET 2		SET 3		SET 4		SET 5		SET 6	
	WT.	REPS.	WT.	REPS.	WT.	REPS.	WT.	REPS.	WT.	REPS.	WT.	REPS.

MUSCLE GROUPS WORKED TODAY: ☐ ARMS ☐ CHEST ☐ BACK ☐ LEGS ☐ CORE ☐ OTHER

MY MOOD TODAY:	TO DO/NOTES:
☐ ☐ ☐	

WEIGHT:

WORKOUT LOG BOOK

DATE:	START:	FINISH:

☐ S ☐ M ☐ T ☐ W ☐ T ☐ F ☐ S ☐ AM ☐ PM ☐ AM ☐ PM

WORKOUT TYPE:	TIME/DISTANCE:	WATER(B OZ GLASSES)	VITAMINS/SUPPLEMENTS
☐ TREADMILL			DOSAGE / QTY.
☐ ELLIPTICAL			
☐ BIKE			
☐ STAIR CLIMBER			
☐ OTHER			
☐ OTHER			

TIME/DISTANCE: **TIME/DISTANCE:**

	TIME/DISTANCE:	TIME/DISTANCE:
☐ RUNNING/JOG		
☐ WALKING		
☐ BIKING		
☐ SWIMMING		
☐ YOGA		
☐ PILATES		
☐ OTHER		
☐ OTHER		

STRENGTH TRAINING

FREE WEIGHTS/ WEIGHT MACHINES:	SET 1		SET 2		SET 3		SET 4		SET 5		SET 6	
	WT.	REPS.	WT.	REPS.	WT.	REPS.	WT.	REPS.	WT.	REPS.	WT.	REPS.

MUSCLE GROUPS WORKED TODAY: ☐ ARMS ☐ CHEST ☐ BACK ☐ LEGS ☐ CORE ☐ OTHER

MY MOOD TODAY:	TO DO/NOTES:
☹ ☐ 😐 ☐ 🙂 ☐	

WEIGHT:

WORKOUT LOG BOOK

DATE:	START:	FINISH:

☐ S ☐ M ☐ T ☐ W ☐ T ☐ F ☐ S   ☐ AM ☐ PM   ☐ AM ☐ PM

WORKOUT TYPE:	TIME/DISTANCE:	WATER(B OZ GLASSES)	VITAMINS/SUPPLEMENTS	
			DOSAGE	QTY.
☐ TREADMILL				
☐ ELLIPTICAL				
☐ BIKE				
☐ STAIR CLIMBER				
☐ OTHER				
☐ OTHER				

TIME/DISTANCE: **TIME/DISTANCE:**

☐ RUNNING/JOG		
☐ WALKING		
☐ BIKING		
☐ SWIMMING		
☐ YOGA		
☐ PILATES		
☐ OTHER		
☐ OTHER		

STRENGTH TRAINING

FREE WEIGHTS/ WEIGHT MACHINES:	SET 1		SET 2		SET 3		SET 4		SET 5		SET 6	
	WT.	REPS.	WT.	REPS.	WT.	REPS.	WT.	REPS.	WT.	REPS.	WT.	REPS.

MUSCLE GROUPS WORKED TODAY: ☐ ARMS ☐ CHEST ☐ BACK ☐ LEGS ☐ CORE ☐ OTHER

MY MOOD TODAY:	TO DO/NOTES:
☐ ☐ ☐	

WEIGHT:

WORKOUT LOG BOOK

DATE:	START:	FINISH:

☐ S ☐ M ☐ T ☐ W ☐ T ☐ F ☐ S   ☐ AM ☐ PM   ☐ AM ☐ PM

WORKOUT TYPE:	TIME/DISTANCE:	WATER(B OZ GLASSES)	VITAMINS/SUPPLEMENTS	
☐ TREADMILL			DOSAGE	QTY.
☐ ELLIPTICAL				
☐ BIKE				
☐ STAIR CLIMBER				
☐ OTHER				
☐ OTHER				

TIME/DISTANCE:		TIME/DISTANCE:				
☐ RUNNING/JOG						
☐ WALKING						
☐ BIKING						
☐ SWIMMING						
☐ YOGA						
☐ PILATES						
☐ OTHER						
☐ OTHER						

STRENGTH TRAINING

FREE WEIGHTS/ WEIGHT MACHINES:	SET 1		SET 2		SET 3		SET 4		SET 5		SET 6	
	WT.	REPS.	WT.	REPS.	WT.	REPS.	WT.	REPS.	WT.	REPS.	WT.	REPS.

MUSCLE GROUPS WORKED TODAY: ☐ ARMS ☐ CHEST ☐ BACK ☐ LEGS ☐ CORE ☐ OTHER

MY MOOD TODAY: **TO DO/NOTES:**

☐   ☐   ☐

WEIGHT:

WORKOUT LOG BOOK

DATE:	START:	FINISH:

☐ S ☐ M ☐ T ☐ W ☐ T ☐ F ☐ S   ☐ AM   ☐ PM   ☐ AM   ☐ PM

WORKOUT TYPE:	TIME/DISTANCE:	WATER(B OZ GLASSES)	VITAMINS/SUPPLEMENTS	
			DOSAGE	QTY.
☐ TREADMILL				
☐ ELLIPTICAL				
☐ BIKE				
☐ STAIR CLIMBER				
☐ OTHER				
☐ OTHER				

TIME/DISTANCE:		TIME/DISTANCE:			
☐ RUNNING/JOG					
☐ WALKING					
☐ BIKING					
☐ SWIMMING					
☐ YOGA					
☐ PILATES					
☐ OTHER					
☐ OTHER					

STRENGTH TRAINING

FREE WEIGHTS/ WEIGHT MACHINES:	SET 1		SET 2		SET 3		SET 4		SET 5		SET 6	
	WT.	REPS.	WT.	REPS.	WT.	REPS.	WT.	REPS.	WT.	REPS.	WT.	REPS.

MUSCLE GROUPS WORKED TODAY: ☐ ARMS ☐ CHEST ☐ BACK ☐ LEGS ☐ CORE ☐ OTHER

MY MOOD TODAY:	TO DO/NOTES:
☹ ☐ 😐 ☐ 🙂 ☐	

WEIGHT:

WORKOUT LOG BOOK

DATE:	START:	FINISH:

☐ S ☐ M ☐ T ☐ W ☐ T ☐ F ☐ S   ☐ AM   ☐ PM   ☐ AM   ☐ PM

WORKOUT TYPE:	TIME/DISTANCE:	WATER(B OZ GLASSES)	VITAMINS/SUPPLEMENTS	
			DOSAGE	QTY.
☐ TREADMILL				
☐ ELLIPTICAL				
☐ BIKE				
☐ STAIR CLIMBER				
☐ OTHER				
☐ OTHER				

TIME/DISTANCE: TIME/DISTANCE:

| ☐ RUNNING/JOG |
| ☐ WALKING |
| ☐ BIKING |
| ☐ SWIMMING |
| ☐ YOGA |
| ☐ PILATES |
| ☐ OTHER |
| ☐ OTHER |

STRENGTH TRAINING

FREE WEIGHTS/ WEIGHT MACHINES:	SET 1		SET 2		SET 3		SET 4		SET 5		SET 6	
	WT.	REPS.	WT.	REPS.	WT.	REPS.	WT.	REPS.	WT.	REPS.	WT.	REPS.

MUSCLE GROUPS WORKED TODAY: ☐ ARMS ☐ CHEST ☐ BACK ☐ LEGS ☐ CORE ☐ OTHER

MY MOOD TODAY: TO DO/NOTES:

☐   ☐   ☐

WEIGHT:

WORKOUT LOG BOOK

DATE:	START:	FINISH:

☐ S ☐ M ☐ T ☐ W ☐ T ☐ F ☐ S   ☐ AM ☐ PM   ☐ AM ☐ PM

WORKOUT TYPE:	TIME/DISTANCE:	WATER(B OZ GLASSES)	VITAMINS/SUPPLEMENTS		
				DOSAGE	QTY.
☐ TREADMILL					
☐ ELLIPTICAL					
☐ BIKE					
☐ STAIR CLIMBER					
☐ OTHER					
☐ OTHER					

TIME/DISTANCE: **TIME/DISTANCE:**

☐ RUNNING/JOG				
☐ WALKING				
☐ BIKING				
☐ SWIMMING				
☐ YOGA				
☐ PILATES				
☐ OTHER				
☐ OTHER				

STRENGTH TRAINING

FREE WEIGHTS/ WEIGHT MACHINES:	SET 1		SET 2		SET 3		SET 4		SET 5		SET 6	
	WT.	REPS.	WT.	REPS.	WT.	REPS.	WT.	REPS.	WT.	REPS.	WT.	REPS.

MUSCLE GROUPS WORKED TODAY: ☐ ARMS ☐ CHEST ☐ BACK ☐ LEGS ☐ CORE ☐ OTHER

MY MOOD TODAY:	TO DO/NOTES:
☹ ☐ 😐 ☐ 🙂 ☐	

WEIGHT:

WORKOUT LOG BOOK

DATE:	START:	FINISH:

☐ S ☐ M ☐ T ☐ W ☐ T ☐ F ☐ S   ☐ AM   ☐ PM   ☐ AM   ☐ PM

WORKOUT TYPE:	TIME/DISTANCE:	WATER(B OZ GLASSES)	VITAMINS/SUPPLEMENTS	
			DOSAGE	QTY.
☐ TREADMILL				
☐ ELLIPTICAL				
☐ BIKE				
☐ STAIR CLIMBER				
☐ OTHER				
☐ OTHER				

TIME/DISTANCE:

TIME/DISTANCE:

☐ RUNNING/JOG					
☐ WALKING					
☐ BIKING					
☐ SWIMMING					
☐ YOGA					
☐ PILATES					
☐ OTHER					
☐ OTHER					

STRENGTH TRAINING

FREE WEIGHTS/ WEIGHT MACHINES:	SET 1		SET 2		SET 3		SET 4		SET 5		SET 6	
	WT.	REPS.	WT.	REPS.	WT.	REPS.	WT.	REPS.	WT.	REPS.	WT.	REPS.

MUSCLE GROUPS WORKED TODAY: ☐ ARMS ☐ CHEST ☐ BACK ☐ LEGS ☐ CORE ☐ OTHER

MY MOOD TODAY:	TO DO/NOTES:
☐ ☐ ☐	

WEIGHT:

WORKOUT LOG BOOK

DATE:	START:	FINISH:

☐ S ☐ M ☐ T ☐ W ☐ T ☐ F ☐ S   ☐ AM   ☐ PM   ☐ AM   ☐ PM

WORKOUT TYPE:	TIME/DISTANCE:	WATER(B OZ GLASSES)	VITAMINS/SUPPLEMENTS	
			DOSAGE	QTY.
☐ TREADMILL				
☐ ELLIPTICAL				
☐ BIKE				
☐ STAIR CLIMBER				
☐ OTHER				
☐ OTHER				

TIME/DISTANCE: **TIME/DISTANCE:**

☐ RUNNING/JOG					
☐ WALKING					
☐ BIKING					
☐ SWIMMING					
☐ YOGA					
☐ PILATES					
☐ OTHER					
☐ OTHER					

STRENGTH TRAINING

FREE WEIGHTS/ WEIGHT MACHINES:	SET 1		SET 2		SET 3		SET 4		SET 5		SET 6	
	WT.	REPS.	WT.	REPS.	WT.	REPS.	WT.	REPS.	WT.	REPS.	WT.	REPS.

MUSCLE GROUPS WORKED TODAY: ☐ ARMS ☐ CHEST ☐ BACK ☐ LEGS ☐ CORE ☐ OTHER

MY MOOD TODAY:	TO DO/NOTES:
☹ ☐ 😐 ☐ 🙂 ☐	

WEIGHT:

WORKOUT LOG BOOK

DATE:	START:	FINISH:

☐S ☐M ☐T ☐W ☐T ☐F ☐S   ☐AM   ☐PM   ☐AM   ☐PM

WORKOUT TYPE:	TIME/DISTANCE:	WATER(B OZ GLASSES)	VITAMINS/SUPPLEMENTS	
			DOSAGE	QTY.
☐ TREADMILL				
☐ ELLIPTICAL				
☐ BIKE				
☐ STAIR CLIMBER				
☐ OTHER				
☐ OTHER				

TIME/DISTANCE:

TIME/DISTANCE:

☐ RUNNING/JOG							
☐ WALKING							
☐ BIKING							
☐ SWIMMING							
☐ YOGA							
☐ PILATES							
☐ OTHER							
☐ OTHER							

STRENGTH TRAINING

FREE WEIGHTS/ WEIGHT MACHINES:	SET 1		SET 2		SET 3		SET 4		SET 5		SET 6	
	WT.	REPS.	WT.	REPS.	WT.	REPS.	WT.	REPS.	WT.	REPS.	WT.	REPS.

MUSCLE GROUPS WORKED TODAY: ☐ARMS ☐CHEST ☐BACK ☐LEGS ☐CORE ☐OTHER

MY MOOD TODAY:	TO DO/NOTES:
☹ ☐ 😐 ☐ 🙂 ☐	

WEIGHT:

WORKOUT LOG BOOK

DATE:	START:	FINISH:

☐ S ☐ M ☐ T ☐ W ☐ T ☐ F ☐ S   ☐ AM   ☐ PM   ☐ AM   ☐ PM

WORKOUT TYPE:	TIME/DISTANCE:	WATER(B OZ GLASSES)	VITAMINS/SUPPLEMENTS	
			DOSAGE	QTY.
☐ TREADMILL				
☐ ELLIPTICAL				
☐ BIKE				
☐ STAIR CLIMBER				
☐ OTHER				
☐ OTHER				

TIME/DISTANCE: **TIME/DISTANCE:**

☐ RUNNING/JOG					
☐ WALKING					
☐ BIKING					
☐ SWIMMING					
☐ YOGA					
☐ PILATES					
☐ OTHER					
☐ OTHER					

STRENGTH TRAINING

FREE WEIGHTS/ WEIGHT MACHINES:	SET 1		SET 2		SET 3		SET 4		SET 5		SET 6	
	WT.	REPS.	WT.	REPS.	WT.	REPS.	WT.	REPS.	WT.	REPS.	WT.	REPS.

MUSCLE GROUPS WORKED TODAY: ☐ ARMS ☐ CHEST ☐ BACK ☐ LEGS ☐ CORE ☐ OTHER

MY MOOD TODAY:	TO DO/NOTES:
☹ ☐ 😐 ☐ 🙂 ☐	

WEIGHT:

WORKOUT LOG BOOK

DATE:	START:	FINISH:

☐ S ☐ M ☐ T ☐ W ☐ T ☐ F ☐ S   ☐ AM   ☐ PM   ☐ AM   ☐ PM

WORKOUT TYPE:	TIME/DISTANCE:	WATER (B OZ GLASSES)	VITAMINS/SUPPLEMENTS	
			DOSAGE	QTY.
☐ TREADMILL				
☐ ELLIPTICAL				
☐ BIKE				
☐ STAIR CLIMBER				
☐ OTHER				
☐ OTHER				

TIME/DISTANCE: / **TIME/DISTANCE:**

☐ RUNNING/JOG					
☐ WALKING					
☐ BIKING					
☐ SWIMMING					
☐ YOGA					
☐ PILATES					
☐ OTHER					
☐ OTHER					

STRENGTH TRAINING

FREE WEIGHTS/ WEIGHT MACHINES:	SET 1		SET 2		SET 3		SET 4		SET 5		SET 6	
	WT.	REPS.	WT.	REPS.	WT.	REPS.	WT.	REPS.	WT.	REPS.	WT.	REPS.

MUSCLE GROUPS WORKED TODAY: ☐ ARMS ☐ CHEST ☐ BACK ☐ LEGS ☐ CORE ☐ OTHER

MY MOOD TODAY:	TO DO/NOTES:
☹ ☐ 😐 ☐ 🙂 ☐	

WEIGHT:	

WORKOUT LOG BOOK

DATE:	START:	FINISH:

☐ S ☐ M ☐ T ☐ W ☐ T ☐ F ☐ S   ☐ AM ☐ PM   ☐ AM ☐ PM

WORKOUT TYPE:	TIME/DISTANCE:	WATER(B OZ GLASSES)	VITAMINS/SUPPLEMENTS	
☐ TREADMILL				DOSAGE	QTY.
☐ ELLIPTICAL				
☐ BIKE				
☐ STAIR CLIMBER				
☐ OTHER				
☐ OTHER				

TIME/DISTANCE:

TIME/DISTANCE:

☐ RUNNING/JOG	
☐ WALKING	
☐ BIKING	
☐ SWIMMING	
☐ YOGA	
☐ PILATES	
☐ OTHER	
☐ OTHER	

STRENGTH TRAINING

FREE WEIGHTS/ WEIGHT MACHINES:	SET 1		SET 2		SET 3		SET 4		SET 5		SET 6	
	WT.	REPS.	WT.	REPS.	WT.	REPS.	WT.	REPS.	WT.	REPS.	WT.	REPS.

MUSCLE GROUPS WORKED TODAY: ☐ ARMS ☐ CHEST ☐ BACK ☐ LEGS ☐ CORE ☐ OTHER

MY MOOD TODAY:

☐   ☐   ☐

TO DO/NOTES:

WEIGHT:

WORKOUT LOG BOOK

DATE:	START:	FINISH:

☐S ☐M ☐T ☐W ☐T ☐F ☐S   ☐AM ☐PM   ☐AM ☐PM

WORKOUT TYPE:	TIME/DISTANCE:	WATER(B OZ GLASSES)	VITAMINS/SUPPLEMENTS	
☐ TREADMILL				DOSAGE	QTY.
☐ ELLIPTICAL				
☐ BIKE				
☐ STAIR CLIMBER				
☐ OTHER				
☐ OTHER				

TIME/DISTANCE:

TIME/DISTANCE:

| ☐ RUNNING/JOG |
| ☐ WALKING |
| ☐ BIKING |
| ☐ SWIMMING |
| ☐ YOGA |
| ☐ PILATES |
| ☐ OTHER |
| ☐ OTHER |

STRENGTH TRAINING

FREE WEIGHTS/ WEIGHT MACHINES:	SET 1		SET 2		SET 3		SET 4		SET 5		SET 6	
	WT.	REPS.	WT.	REPS.	WT.	REPS.	WT.	REPS.	WT.	REPS.	WT.	REPS.

MUSCLE GROUPS WORKED TODAY: ☐ARMS ☐CHEST ☐BACK ☐LEGS ☐CORE ☐OTHER

MY MOOD TODAY:	TO DO/NOTES:
☹ ☐ 😐 ☐ ☺ ☐	

WEIGHT:

WORKOUT LOG BOOK

DATE:	START:	FINISH:

☐ S ☐ M ☐ T ☐ W ☐ T ☐ F ☐ S   ☐ AM   ☐ PM   ☐ AM   ☐ PM

WORKOUT TYPE:	TIME/DISTANCE:	WATER(B OZ GLASSES)	VITAMINS/SUPPLEMENTS	
			DOSAGE	QTY.
☐ TREADMILL				
☐ ELLIPTICAL				
☐ BIKE				
☐ STAIR CLIMBER				
☐ OTHER				
☐ OTHER				

TIME/DISTANCE: **TIME/DISTANCE:**

- ☐ RUNNING/JOG
- ☐ WALKING
- ☐ BIKING
- ☐ SWIMMING
- ☐ YOGA
- ☐ PILATES
- ☐ OTHER
- ☐ OTHER

STRENGTH TRAINING

FREE WEIGHTS/ WEIGHT MACHINES:	SET 1		SET 2		SET 3		SET 4		SET 5		SET 6	
	WT.	REPS.	WT.	REPS.	WT.	REPS.	WT.	REPS.	WT.	REPS.	WT.	REPS.

MUSCLE GROUPS WORKED TODAY: ☐ ARMS ☐ CHEST ☐ BACK ☐ LEGS ☐ CORE ☐ OTHER

MY MOOD TODAY:	TO DO/NOTES:
☐ ☐ ☐	

WEIGHT:

WORKOUT LOG BOOK

DATE:	START:	FINISH:

☐ S ☐ M ☐ T ☐ W ☐ T ☐ F ☐ S   ☐ AM   ☐ PM   ☐ AM   ☐ PM

WORKOUT TYPE:	TIME/DISTANCE:	WATER(B OZ GLASSES)	VITAMINS/SUPPLEMENTS	
			DOSAGE	QTY.
☐ TREADMILL				
☐ ELLIPTICAL				
☐ BIKE				
☐ STAIR CLIMBER				
☐ OTHER				
☐ OTHER				

TIME/DISTANCE: **TIME/DISTANCE:**

☐ RUNNING/JOG	
☐ WALKING	
☐ BIKING	
☐ SWIMMING	
☐ YOGA	
☐ PILATES	
☐ OTHER	
☐ OTHER	

STRENGTH TRAINING

FREE WEIGHTS/ WEIGHT MACHINES:	SET 1		SET 2		SET 3		SET 4		SET 5		SET 6	
	WT.	REPS.	WT.	REPS.	WT.	REPS.	WT.	REPS.	WT.	REPS.	WT.	REPS.

MUSCLE GROUPS WORKED TODAY: ☐ ARMS ☐ CHEST ☐ BACK ☐ LEGS ☐ CORE ☐ OTHER

MY MOOD TODAY: **TO DO/NOTES:**

☐   ☐   ☐

WEIGHT:

WORKOUT LOG BOOK

DATE:	START:	FINISH:

☐ S ☐ M ☐ T ☐ W ☐ T ☐ F ☐ S   ☐ AM   ☐ PM   ☐ AM   ☐ PM

WORKOUT TYPE:	TIME/DISTANCE:	WATER(B OZ GLASSES)	VITAMINS/SUPPLEMENTS	
			DOSAGE	QTY.
☐ TREADMILL				
☐ ELLIPTICAL				
☐ BIKE				
☐ STAIR CLIMBER				
☐ OTHER				
☐ OTHER				

TIME/DISTANCE: **TIME/DISTANCE:**

☐ RUNNING/JOG						
☐ WALKING						
☐ BIKING						
☐ SWIMMING						
☐ YOGA						
☐ PILATES						
☐ OTHER						
☐ OTHER						

STRENGTH TRAINING

FREE WEIGHTS/ WEIGHT MACHINES:	SET 1		SET 2		SET 3		SET 4		SET 5		SET 6	
	WT.	REPS.	WT.	REPS.	WT.	REPS.	WT.	REPS.	WT.	REPS.	WT.	REPS.

MUSCLE GROUPS WORKED TODAY: ☐ ARMS ☐ CHEST ☐ BACK ☐ LEGS ☐ CORE ☐ OTHER

MY MOOD TODAY: **TO DO/NOTES:**

☐   ☐   ☐

WEIGHT:

WORKOUT LOG BOOK

<table>
<tr><td>DATE:</td><td>START:</td><td>FINISH:</td></tr>
</table>

☐ S ☐ M ☐ T ☐ W ☐ T ☐ F ☐ S   ☐ AM   ☐ PM   ☐ AM   ☐ PM

WORKOUT TYPE:	TIME/DISTANCE:	WATER(B OZ GLASSES)	VITAMINS/SUPPLEMENTS	
			DOSAGE	QTY.
☐ TREADMILL				
☐ ELLIPTICAL				
☐ BIKE				
☐ STAIR CLIMBER				
☐ OTHER				
☐ OTHER				

TIME/DISTANCE: **TIME/DISTANCE:**

RUNNING/JOG						
☐ RUNNING/JOG						
☐ WALKING						
☐ BIKING						
☐ SWIMMING						
☐ YOGA						
☐ PILATES						
☐ OTHER						
☐ OTHER						

STRENGTH TRAINING

FREE WEIGHTS/ WEIGHT MACHINES:	SET 1		SET 2		SET 3		SET 4		SET 5		SET 6	
	WT.	REPS.	WT.	REPS.	WT.	REPS.	WT.	REPS.	WT.	REPS.	WT.	REPS.

MUSCLE GROUPS WORKED TODAY: ☐ ARMS ☐ CHEST ☐ BACK ☐ LEGS ☐ CORE ☐ OTHER

MY MOOD TODAY: **TO DO/NOTES:**

☐   ☐   ☐

WEIGHT:

WORKOUT LOG BOOK

DATE:	START:	FINISH:

☐ S ☐ M ☐ T ☐ W ☐ T ☐ F ☐ S ☐ AM ☐ PM ☐ AM ☐ PM

WORKOUT TYPE:	TIME/DISTANCE:	WATER(B OZ GLASSES)	VITAMINS/SUPPLEMENTS	
			DOSAGE	QTY.
☐ TREADMILL				
☐ ELLIPTICAL				
☐ BIKE				
☐ STAIR CLIMBER				
☐ OTHER				
☐ OTHER				

TIME/DISTANCE: **TIME/DISTANCE:**

☐ RUNNING/JOG					
☐ WALKING					
☐ BIKING					
☐ SWIMMING					
☐ YOGA					
☐ PILATES					
☐ OTHER					
☐ OTHER					

STRENGTH TRAINING

FREE WEIGHTS/ WEIGHT MACHINES:	SET 1		SET 2		SET 3		SET 4		SET 5		SET 6	
	WT.	REPS.	WT.	REPS.	WT.	REPS.	WT.	REPS.	WT.	REPS.	WT.	REPS.

MUSCLE GROUPS WORKED TODAY: ☐ ARMS ☐ CHEST ☐ BACK ☐ LEGS ☐ CORE ☐ OTHER

MY MOOD TODAY:	TO DO/NOTES:
☹ ☐ 😐 ☐ 🙂 ☐	

WEIGHT:

WORKOUT LOG BOOK

DATE:	START:	FINISH:

☐ S ☐ M ☐ T ☐ W ☐ T ☐ F ☐ S　　　☐ AM　☐ PM　　　　☐ AM　☐ PM

WORKOUT TYPE:	TIME/DISTANCE:	WATER(B OZ GLASSES)	VITAMINS/SUPPLEMENTS	
			DOSAGE	QTY.
☐ TREADMILL				
☐ ELLIPTICAL				
☐ BIKE				
☐ STAIR CLIMBER				
☐ OTHER				
☐ OTHER				

TIME/DISTANCE:　　　　**TIME/DISTANCE:**

☐ RUNNING/JOG						
☐ WALKING						
☐ BIKING						
☐ SWIMMING						
☐ YOGA						
☐ PILATES						
☐ OTHER						
☐ OTHER						

STRENGTH TRAINING

FREE WEIGHTS/ WEIGHT MACHINES:	SET 1		SET 2		SET 3		SET 4		SET 5		SET 6	
	WT.	REPS.	WT.	REPS.	WT.	REPS.	WT.	REPS.	WT.	REPS.	WT.	REPS.

MUSCLE GROUPS WORKED TODAY:　☐ ARMS ☐ CHEST ☐ BACK ☐ LEGS ☐ CORE ☐ OTHER

MY MOOD TODAY:

TO DO/NOTES:

☐　　☐　　☐

WEIGHT:

WORKOUT LOG BOOK

DATE:	START:	FINISH:

☐ S ☐ M ☐ T ☐ W ☐ T ☐ F ☐ S   ☐ AM   ☐ PM   ☐ AM   ☐ PM

WORKOUT TYPE:	TIME/DISTANCE:	WATER(B OZ GLASSES)	VITAMINS/SUPPLEMENTS	
			DOSAGE	QTY.
☐ TREADMILL				
☐ ELLIPTICAL				
☐ BIKE				
☐ STAIR CLIMBER				
☐ OTHER				
☐ OTHER				

TIME/DISTANCE: **TIME/DISTANCE:**

☐ RUNNING/JOG					
☐ WALKING					
☐ BIKING					
☐ SWIMMING					
☐ YOGA					
☐ PILATES					
☐ OTHER					
☐ OTHER					

STRENGTH TRAINING

FREE WEIGHTS/ WEIGHT MACHINES:	SET 1		SET 2		SET 3		SET 4		SET 5		SET 6	
	WT.	REPS.	WT.	REPS.	WT.	REPS.	WT.	REPS.	WT.	REPS.	WT.	REPS.

MUSCLE GROUPS WORKED TODAY: ☐ ARMS ☐ CHEST ☐ BACK ☐ LEGS ☐ CORE ☐ OTHER

MY MOOD TODAY: **TO DO/NOTES:**

☐   ☐   ☐

WEIGHT:

WORKOUT LOG BOOK

DATE:	START:	FINISH:

☐ S ☐ M ☐ T ☐ W ☐ T ☐ F ☐ S   ☐ AM ☐ PM   ☐ AM ☐ PM

WORKOUT TYPE:	TIME/DISTANCE:	WATER(B OZ GLASSES)	VITAMINS/SUPPLEMENTS	
			DOSAGE	QTY.
☐ TREADMILL				
☐ ELLIPTICAL				
☐ BIKE				
☐ STAIR CLIMBER				
☐ OTHER				
☐ OTHER				

TIME/DISTANCE: **TIME/DISTANCE:**

☐ RUNNING/JOG				
☐ WALKING				
☐ BIKING				
☐ SWIMMING				
☐ YOGA				
☐ PILATES				
☐ OTHER				
☐ OTHER				

STRENGTH TRAINING

FREE WEIGHTS/ WEIGHT MACHINES:	SET 1		SET 2		SET 3		SET 4		SET 5		SET 6	
	WT.	REPS.	WT.	REPS.	WT.	REPS.	WT.	REPS.	WT.	REPS.	WT.	REPS.

MUSCLE GROUPS WORKED TODAY: ☐ ARMS ☐ CHEST ☐ BACK ☐ LEGS ☐ CORE ☐ OTHER

MY MOOD TODAY: **TO DO/NOTES:**

☐   ☐   ☐

WEIGHT:

WORKOUT LOG BOOK

DATE:	START:	FINISH:

☐ S ☐ M ☐ T ☐ W ☐ T ☐ F ☐ S   ☐ AM   ☐ PM   ☐ AM   ☐ PM

WORKOUT TYPE:	TIME/DISTANCE:	WATER(B OZ GLASSES)	VITAMINS/SUPPLEMENTS	
			DOSAGE	QTY.
☐ TREADMILL				
☐ ELLIPTICAL				
☐ BIKE				
☐ STAIR CLIMBER				
☐ OTHER				
☐ OTHER				

TIME/DISTANCE:		TIME/DISTANCE:			
☐ RUNNING/JOG					
☐ WALKING					
☐ BIKING					
☐ SWIMMING					
☐ YOGA					
☐ PILATES					
☐ OTHER					
☐ OTHER					

STRENGTH TRAINING

FREE WEIGHTS/ WEIGHT MACHINES:	SET 1		SET 2		SET 3		SET 4		SET 5		SET 6	
	WT.	REPS.	WT.	REPS.	WT.	REPS.	WT.	REPS.	WT.	REPS.	WT.	REPS.

MUSCLE GROUPS WORKED TODAY: ☐ ARMS ☐ CHEST ☐ BACK ☐ LEGS ☐ CORE ☐ OTHER

MY MOOD TODAY:	TO DO/NOTES:
☹ ☐ ☺ ☐ ☺ ☐	

WEIGHT:

WORKOUT LOG BOOK

DATE:	START:	FINISH:

☐ S ☐ M ☐ T ☐ W ☐ T ☐ F ☐ S   ☐ AM   ☐ PM   ☐ AM   ☐ PM

WORKOUT TYPE:	TIME/DISTANCE:	WATER(B OZ GLASSES)	VITAMINS/SUPPLEMENTS	
			DOSAGE	QTY.
☐ TREADMILL				
☐ ELLIPTICAL				
☐ BIKE				
☐ STAIR CLIMBER				
☐ OTHER				
☐ OTHER				

TIME/DISTANCE: **TIME/DISTANCE:**

☐ RUNNING/JOG		
☐ WALKING		
☐ BIKING		
☐ SWIMMING		
☐ YOGA		
☐ PILATES		
☐ OTHER		
☐ OTHER		

STRENGTH TRAINING

FREE WEIGHTS/ WEIGHT MACHINES:	SET 1		SET 2		SET 3		SET 4		SET 5		SET 6	
	WT.	REPS.	WT.	REPS.	WT.	REPS.	WT.	REPS.	WT.	REPS.	WT.	REPS.

MUSCLE GROUPS WORKED TODAY: ☐ ARMS ☐ CHEST ☐ BACK ☐ LEGS ☐ CORE ☐ OTHER

MY MOOD TODAY: **TO DO/NOTES:**

☐   ☐   ☐

WEIGHT:

WORKOUT LOG BOOK

DATE:	START:	FINISH:

☐S ☐M ☐T ☐W ☐T ☐F ☐S   ☐AM ☐PM   ☐AM ☐PM

WORKOUT TYPE:	TIME/DISTANCE:	WATER(B OZ GLASSES)	VITAMINS/SUPPLEMENTS		
				DOSAGE	QTY.
☐ TREADMILL					
☐ ELLIPTICAL					
☐ BIKE					
☐ STAIR CLIMBER					
☐ OTHER					
☐ OTHER					

TIME/DISTANCE: **TIME/DISTANCE:**

☐ RUNNING/JOG					
☐ WALKING					
☐ BIKING					
☐ SWIMMING					
☐ YOGA					
☐ PILATES					
☐ OTHER					
☐ OTHER					

STRENGTH TRAINING

FREE WEIGHTS/ WEIGHT MACHINES:	SET 1		SET 2		SET 3		SET 4		SET 5		SET 6	
	WT.	REPS.	WT.	REPS.	WT.	REPS.	WT.	REPS.	WT.	REPS.	WT.	REPS.

MUSCLE GROUPS WORKED TODAY: ☐ARMS ☐CHEST ☐BACK ☐LEGS ☐CORE ☐OTHER

MY MOOD TODAY:	TO DO/NOTES:
☹ ☐ 😐 ☐ ☺ ☐	

WEIGHT:

WORKOUT LOG BOOK

DATE:	START:	FINISH:

☐ S ☐ M ☐ T ☐ W ☐ T ☐ F ☐ S   ☐ AM   ☐ PM   ☐ AM   ☐ PM

WORKOUT TYPE:	TIME/DISTANCE:	WATER(B OZ GLASSES)	VITAMINS/SUPPLEMENTS	
			DOSAGE	QTY.
☐ TREADMILL				
☐ ELLIPTICAL				
☐ BIKE				
☐ STAIR CLIMBER				
☐ OTHER				
☐ OTHER				

TIME/DISTANCE: **TIME/DISTANCE:**

RUNNING/JOG	WALKING	BIKING	SWIMMING	YOGA	PILATES	OTHER	OTHER
☐	☐	☐	☐	☐	☐	☐	☐

STRENGTH TRAINING

FREE WEIGHTS/ WEIGHT MACHINES:	SET 1		SET 2		SET 3		SET 4		SET 5		SET 6	
	WT.	REPS.	WT.	REPS.	WT.	REPS.	WT.	REPS.	WT.	REPS.	WT.	REPS.

MUSCLE GROUPS WORKED TODAY: ☐ ARMS ☐ CHEST ☐ BACK ☐ LEGS ☐ CORE ☐ OTHER

MY MOOD TODAY:	TO DO/NOTES:
☹ ☐ 😐 ☐ 🙂 ☐	

WEIGHT:

WORKOUT LOG BOOK

DATE:	START:	FINISH:

☐ S ☐ M ☐ T ☐ W ☐ T ☐ F ☐ S   ☐ AM   ☐ PM   ☐ AM   ☐ PM

WORKOUT TYPE:	TIME/DISTANCE:	WATER(B OZ GLASSES)	VITAMINS/SUPPLEMENTS	
			DOSAGE	QTY.
☐ TREADMILL				
☐ ELLIPTICAL				
☐ BIKE				
☐ STAIR CLIMBER				
☐ OTHER				
☐ OTHER				

TIME/DISTANCE: **TIME/DISTANCE:**

☐ RUNNING/JOG					
☐ WALKING					
☐ BIKING					
☐ SWIMMING					
☐ YOGA					
☐ PILATES					
☐ OTHER					
☐ OTHER					

STRENGTH TRAINING

FREE WEIGHTS/ WEIGHT MACHINES:	SET 1		SET 2		SET 3		SET 4		SET 5		SET 6	
	WT.	REPS.	WT.	REPS.	WT.	REPS.	WT.	REPS.	WT.	REPS.	WT.	REPS.

MUSCLE GROUPS WORKED TODAY: ☐ ARMS ☐ CHEST ☐ BACK ☐ LEGS ☐ CORE ☐ OTHER

MY MOOD TODAY:	TO DO/NOTES:
☹ ☐ 😐 ☐ 🙂 ☐	

WEIGHT:

WORKOUT LOG BOOK

DATE:	START:	FINISH:

☐ S ☐ M ☐ T ☐ W ☐ T ☐ F ☐ S   ☐ AM   ☐ PM   ☐ AM   ☐ PM

WORKOUT TYPE:	TIME/DISTANCE:	WATER(B OZ GLASSES)	VITAMINS/SUPPLEMENTS	
☐ TREADMILL				DOSAGE	QTY.
☐ ELLIPTICAL				
☐ BIKE				
☐ STAIR CLIMBER				
☐ OTHER				
☐ OTHER				

TIME/DISTANCE:

TIME/DISTANCE:

☐ RUNNING/JOG					
☐ WALKING					
☐ BIKING					
☐ SWIMMING					
☐ YOGA					
☐ PILATES					
☐ OTHER					
☐ OTHER					

STRENGTH TRAINING

FREE WEIGHTS/ WEIGHT MACHINES:	SET 1		SET 2		SET 3		SET 4		SET 5		SET 6	
	WT.	REPS.	WT.	REPS.	WT.	REPS.	WT.	REPS.	WT.	REPS.	WT.	REPS.

MUSCLE GROUPS WORKED TODAY: ☐ ARMS ☐ CHEST ☐ BACK ☐ LEGS ☐ CORE ☐ OTHER

MY MOOD TODAY:	TO DO/NOTES:
☹ ☐ 😐 ☐ 🙂 ☐	

WEIGHT:

WORKOUT LOG BOOK

DATE:	START:	FINISH:

☐ S ☐ M ☐ T ☐ W ☐ T ☐ F ☐ S   ☐ AM   ☐ PM   ☐ AM   ☐ PM

WORKOUT TYPE:	TIME/DISTANCE:	WATER(B OZ GLASSES)	VITAMINS/SUPPLEMENTS	
			DOSAGE	QTY.
☐ TREADMILL				
☐ ELLIPTICAL				
☐ BIKE				
☐ STAIR CLIMBER				
☐ OTHER				
☐ OTHER				

TIME/DISTANCE: **TIME/DISTANCE:**

☐ RUNNING/JOG				
☐ WALKING				
☐ BIKING				
☐ SWIMMING				
☐ YOGA				
☐ PILATES				
☐ OTHER				
☐ OTHER				

STRENGTH TRAINING

FREE WEIGHTS/ WEIGHT MACHINES:	SET 1		SET 2		SET 3		SET 4		SET 5		SET 6	
	WT.	REPS.	WT.	REPS.	WT.	REPS.	WT.	REPS.	WT.	REPS.	WT.	REPS.

MUSCLE GROUPS WORKED TODAY: ☐ ARMS ☐ CHEST ☐ BACK ☐ LEGS ☐ CORE ☐ OTHER

MY MOOD TODAY:	TO DO/NOTES:
☹ ☐ 😐 ☐ ☺ ☐	

WEIGHT:

WORKOUT LOG BOOK

DATE:	START:	FINISH:

☐ S ☐ M ☐ T ☐ W ☐ T ☐ F ☐ S   ☐ AM   ☐ PM   ☐ AM   ☐ PM

WORKOUT TYPE:	TIME/DISTANCE:	WATER (B OZ GLASSES)	VITAMINS/SUPPLEMENTS		
				DOSAGE	QTY.
☐ TREADMILL					
☐ ELLIPTICAL					
☐ BIKE					
☐ STAIR CLIMBER					
☐ OTHER					
☐ OTHER					

TIME/DISTANCE: **TIME/DISTANCE:**

☐ RUNNING/JOG		
☐ WALKING		
☐ BIKING		
☐ SWIMMING		
☐ YOGA		
☐ PILATES		
☐ OTHER		
☐ OTHER		

STRENGTH TRAINING

FREE WEIGHTS/ WEIGHT MACHINES:	SET 1		SET 2		SET 3		SET 4		SET 5		SET 6	
	WT.	REPS.	WT.	REPS.	WT.	REPS.	WT.	REPS.	WT.	REPS.	WT.	REPS.

MUSCLE GROUPS WORKED TODAY: ☐ ARMS ☐ CHEST ☐ BACK ☐ LEGS ☐ CORE ☐ OTHER

MY MOOD TODAY: **TO DO/NOTES:**

☐   ☐   ☐

WEIGHT:

WORKOUT LOG BOOK

DATE:	START:	FINISH:

☐S ☐M ☐T ☐W ☐T ☐F ☐S　　　☐AM　☐PM　　　　☐AM　☐PM

WORKOUT TYPE:	TIME/DISTANCE:	WATER(B OZ GLASSES)	VITAMINS/SUPPLEMENTS	
			DOSAGE	QTY.
☐ TREADMILL				
☐ ELLIPTICAL				
☐ BIKE				
☐ STAIR CLIMBER				
☐ OTHER				
☐ OTHER				

TIME/DISTANCE:　　　　　　　　**TIME/DISTANCE:**

☐ RUNNING/JOG				
☐ WALKING				
☐ BIKING				
☐ SWIMMING				
☐ YOGA				
☐ PILATES				
☐ OTHER				
☐ OTHER				

STRENGTH TRAINING

FREE WEIGHTS/ WEIGHT MACHINES:	SET 1		SET 2		SET 3		SET 4		SET 5		SET 6	
	WT.	REPS.	WT.	REPS.	WT.	REPS.	WT.	REPS.	WT.	REPS.	WT.	REPS.

MUSCLE GROUPS WORKED TODAY:　☐ARMS ☐CHEST ☐BACK ☐LEGS ☐CORE ☐OTHER

MY MOOD TODAY:	TO DO/NOTES:
☐　　☐　　☐	

WEIGHT:

WORKOUT LOG BOOK

DATE:	START:	FINISH:

☐S ☐M ☐T ☐W ☐T ☐F ☐S   ☐AM   ☐PM   ☐AM   ☐PM

WORKOUT TYPE:	TIME/DISTANCE:	WATER(B OZ GLASSES)	VITAMINS/SUPPLEMENTS	
☐ TREADMILL				DOSAGE	QTY.
☐ ELLIPTICAL				
☐ BIKE				
☐ STAIR CLIMBER				
☐ OTHER				
☐ OTHER				

TIME/DISTANCE:		TIME/DISTANCE:					
☐ RUNNING/JOG							
☐ WALKING							
☐ BIKING							
☐ SWIMMING							
☐ YOGA							
☐ PILATES							
☐ OTHER							
☐ OTHER							

STRENGTH TRAINING

FREE WEIGHTS/ WEIGHT MACHINES:	SET 1		SET 2		SET 3		SET 4		SET 5		SET 6	
	WT.	REPS.	WT.	REPS.	WT.	REPS.	WT.	REPS.	WT.	REPS.	WT.	REPS.

MUSCLE GROUPS WORKED TODAY: ☐ARMS ☐CHEST ☐BACK ☐LEGS ☐CORE ☐OTHER

MY MOOD TODAY:	TO DO/NOTES:
☐ ☐ ☐	

WEIGHT:

WORKOUT LOG BOOK

DATE:	START:	FINISH:

☐S ☐M ☐T ☐W ☐T ☐F ☐S   ☐AM ☐PM   ☐AM ☐PM

WORKOUT TYPE:	TIME/DISTANCE:	WATER(B OZ GLASSES)	VITAMINS/SUPPLEMENTS	
			DOSAGE	QTY.
☐ TREADMILL				
☐ ELLIPTICAL				
☐ BIKE				
☐ STAIR CLIMBER				
☐ OTHER				
☐ OTHER				

TIME/DISTANCE:

TIME/DISTANCE:

☐ RUNNING/JOG					
☐ WALKING					
☐ BIKING					
☐ SWIMMING					
☐ YOGA					
☐ PILATES					
☐ OTHER					
☐ OTHER					

STRENGTH TRAINING

FREE WEIGHTS/ WEIGHT MACHINES:	SET 1		SET 2		SET 3		SET 4		SET 5		SET 6	
	WT.	REPS.	WT.	REPS.	WT.	REPS.	WT.	REPS.	WT.	REPS.	WT.	REPS.

MUSCLE GROUPS WORKED TODAY: ☐ARMS ☐CHEST ☐BACK ☐LEGS ☐CORE ☐OTHER

MY MOOD TODAY:	TO DO/NOTES:
☐ ☐ ☐	

WEIGHT:

WORKOUT LOG BOOK

DATE:	START:	FINISH:

☐ S ☐ M ☐ T ☐ W ☐ T ☐ F ☐ S   ☐ AM   ☐ PM   ☐ AM   ☐ PM

WORKOUT TYPE:	TIME/DISTANCE:	WATER(B OZ GLASSES)	VITAMINS/SUPPLEMENTS	
			DOSAGE	QTY.
☐ TREADMILL				
☐ ELLIPTICAL				
☐ BIKE				
☐ STAIR CLIMBER				
☐ OTHER				
☐ OTHER				

TIME/DISTANCE:		TIME/DISTANCE:					
☐ RUNNING/JOG							
☐ WALKING							
☐ BIKING							
☐ SWIMMING							
☐ YOGA							
☐ PILATES							
☐ OTHER							
☐ OTHER							

STRENGTH TRAINING

FREE WEIGHTS/ WEIGHT MACHINES:	SET 1		SET 2		SET 3		SET 4		SET 5		SET 6	
	WT.	REPS.	WT.	REPS.	WT.	REPS.	WT.	REPS.	WT.	REPS.	WT.	REPS.

MUSCLE GROUPS WORKED TODAY: ☐ ARMS ☐ CHEST ☐ BACK ☐ LEGS ☐ CORE ☐ OTHER

MY MOOD TODAY:	TO DO/NOTES:
☹ ☐ 😐 ☐ ☺ ☐	

WEIGHT:

www.ingramcontent.com/pod-product-compliance
Lightning Source LLC
Chambersburg PA
CBHW051431150726
48000CB00005B/2051